I0391037

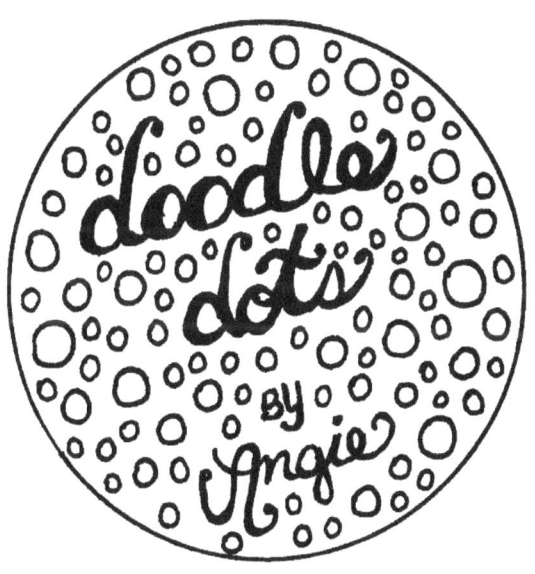

Doodle Dots and Designs

A Detailed Adult Coloring Book

By Angie Thompson

Acknowledgements

I'd like to lovingly acknowledge my son, Gene and my fiancé, Gil for their love, patience and support as I reach out to achieve a dream. You guys are my world, forever. Love you to the moon and back!!!

I'd like to thank my friends who have listened to me, shared their opinions with me and provided me with encouragement. You ladies amaze me every day! I would especially like to send extra love to my bestie, Venessa. You. Are. Awesome.

Thanks to Alisann Smookler, a favorite independent artist, who was willing to help out in me learning independent publishing! Thank you for helping another artist grow.

Love to my Aunt Merle Lee who has inspired me with her passion for art and books my whole life.

Last but not least, my Mom, Dad and Sister, Sarah. Your unconditional love has made me a better person.

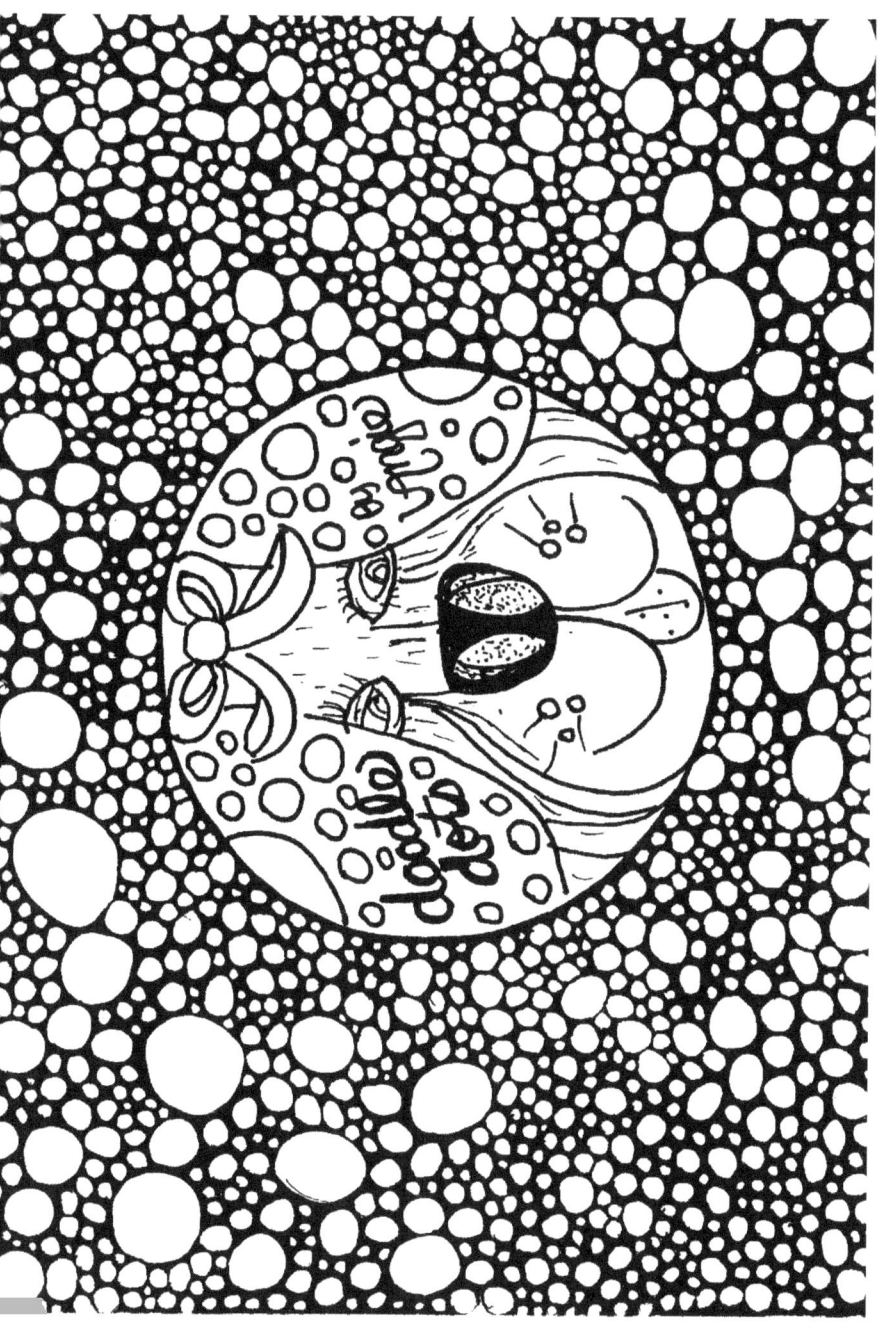

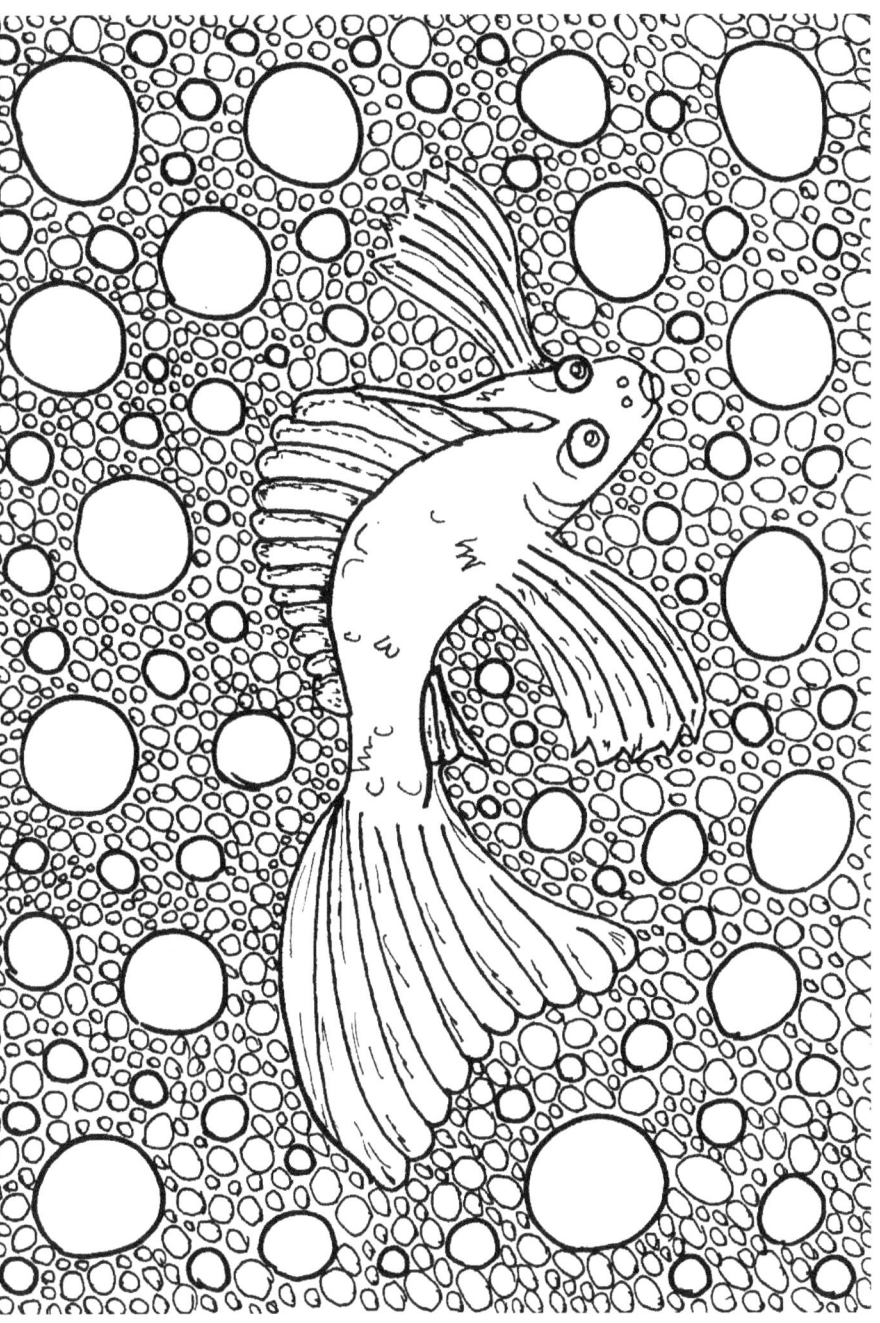

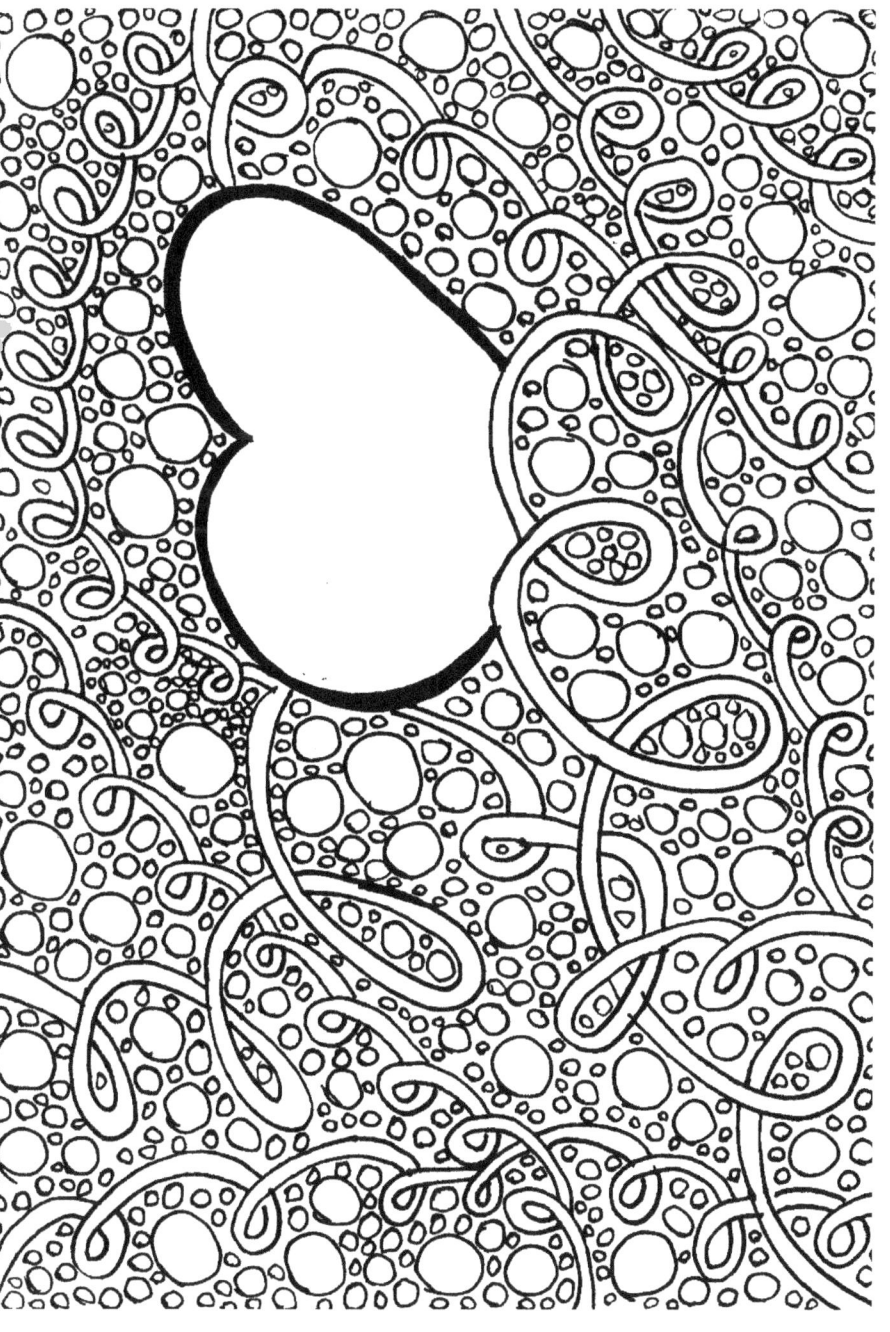

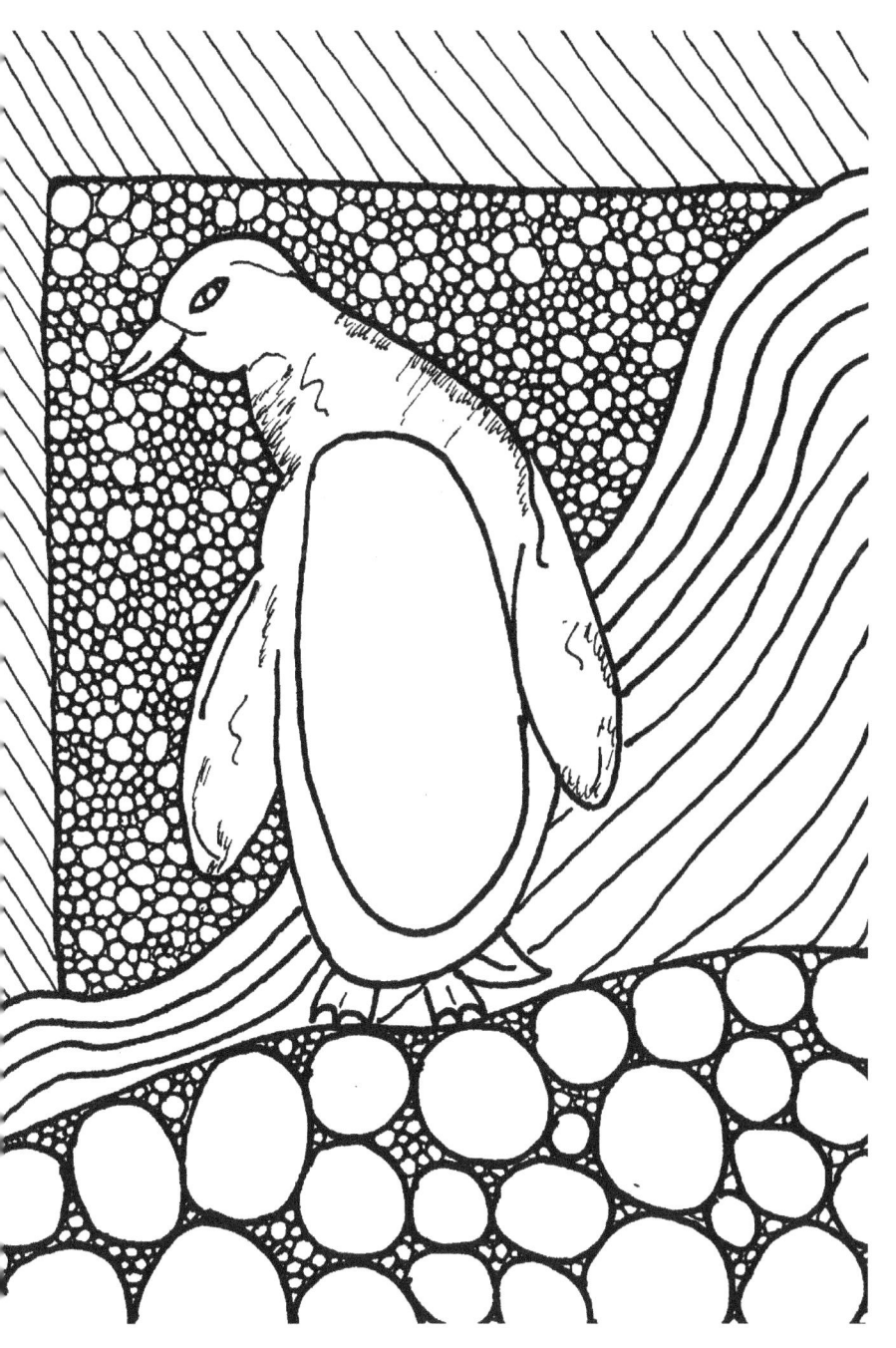

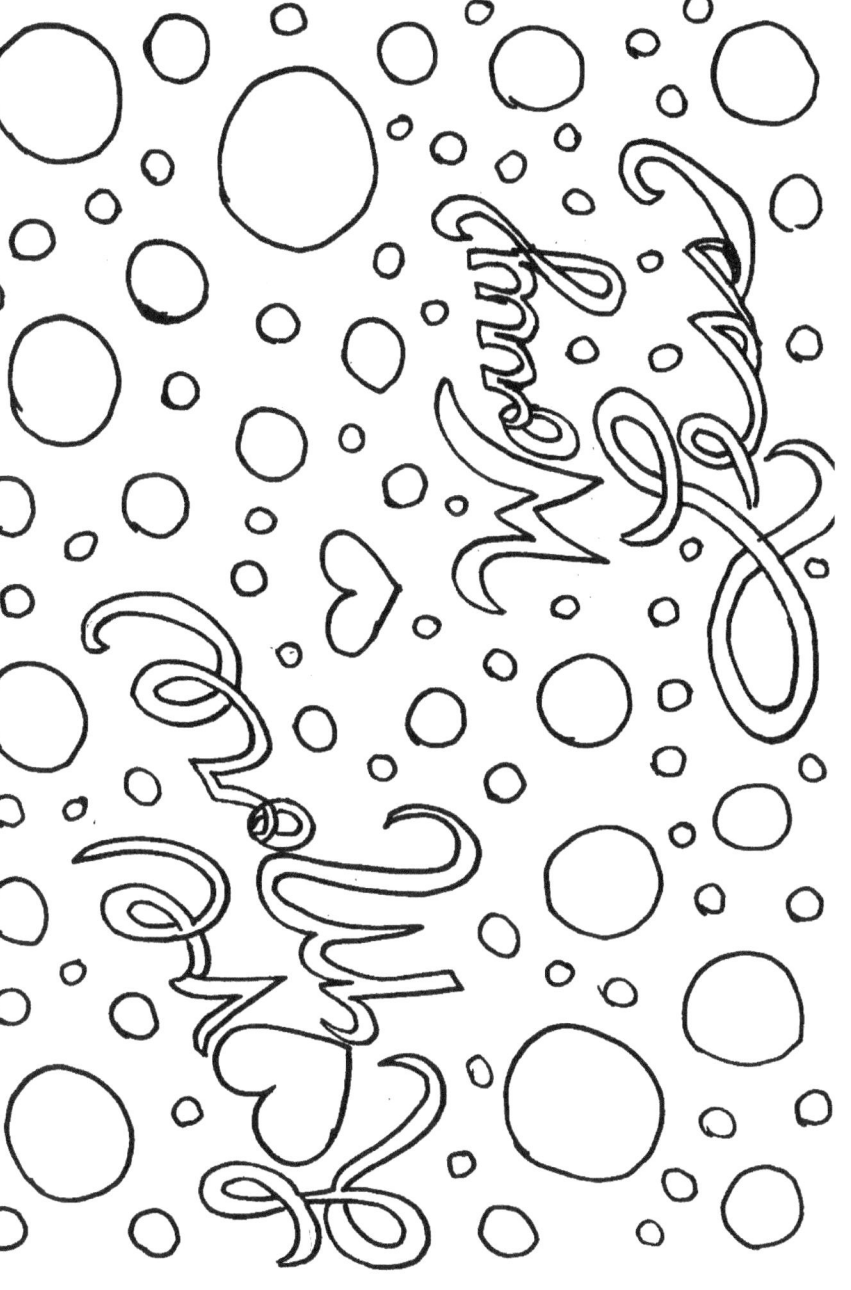

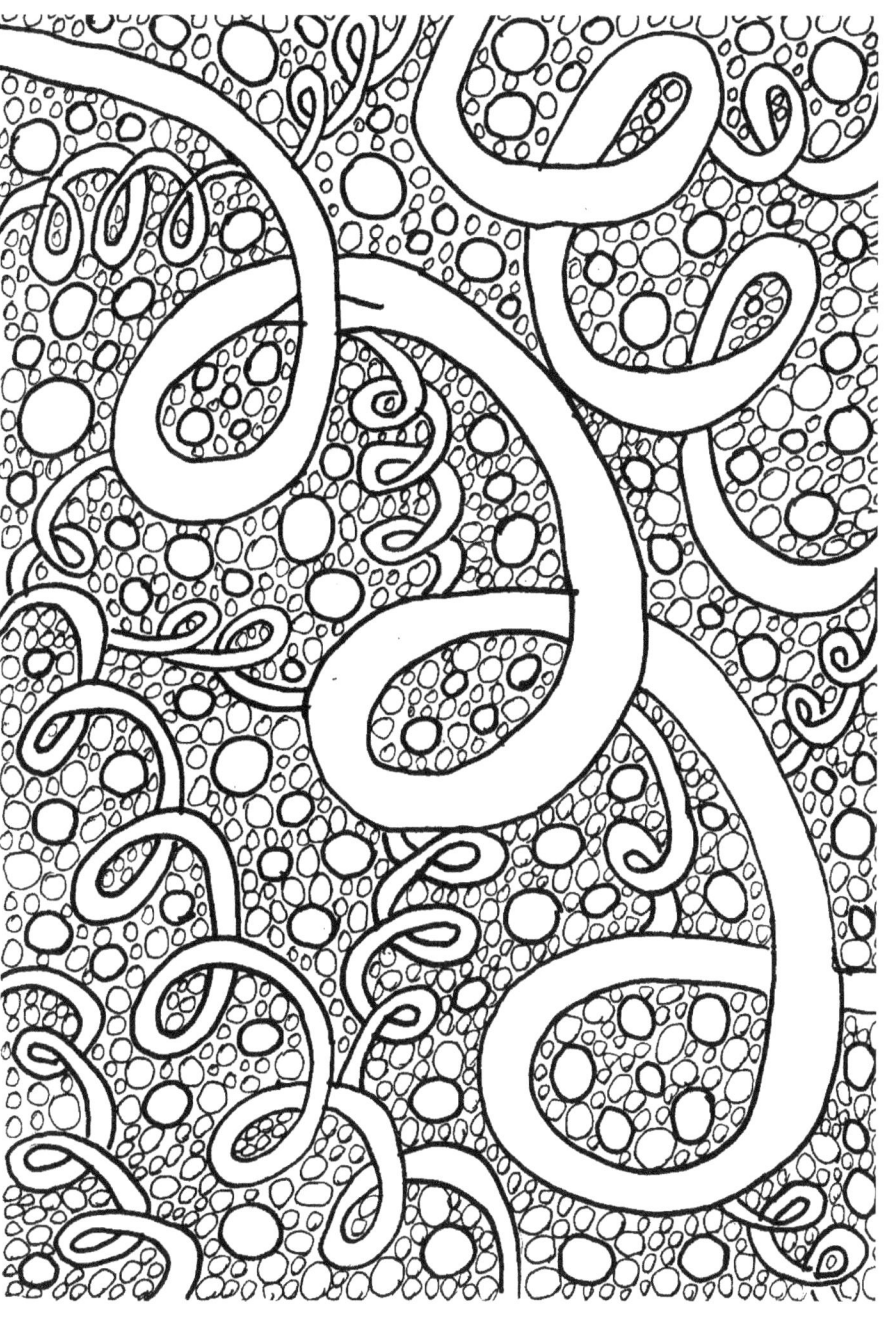

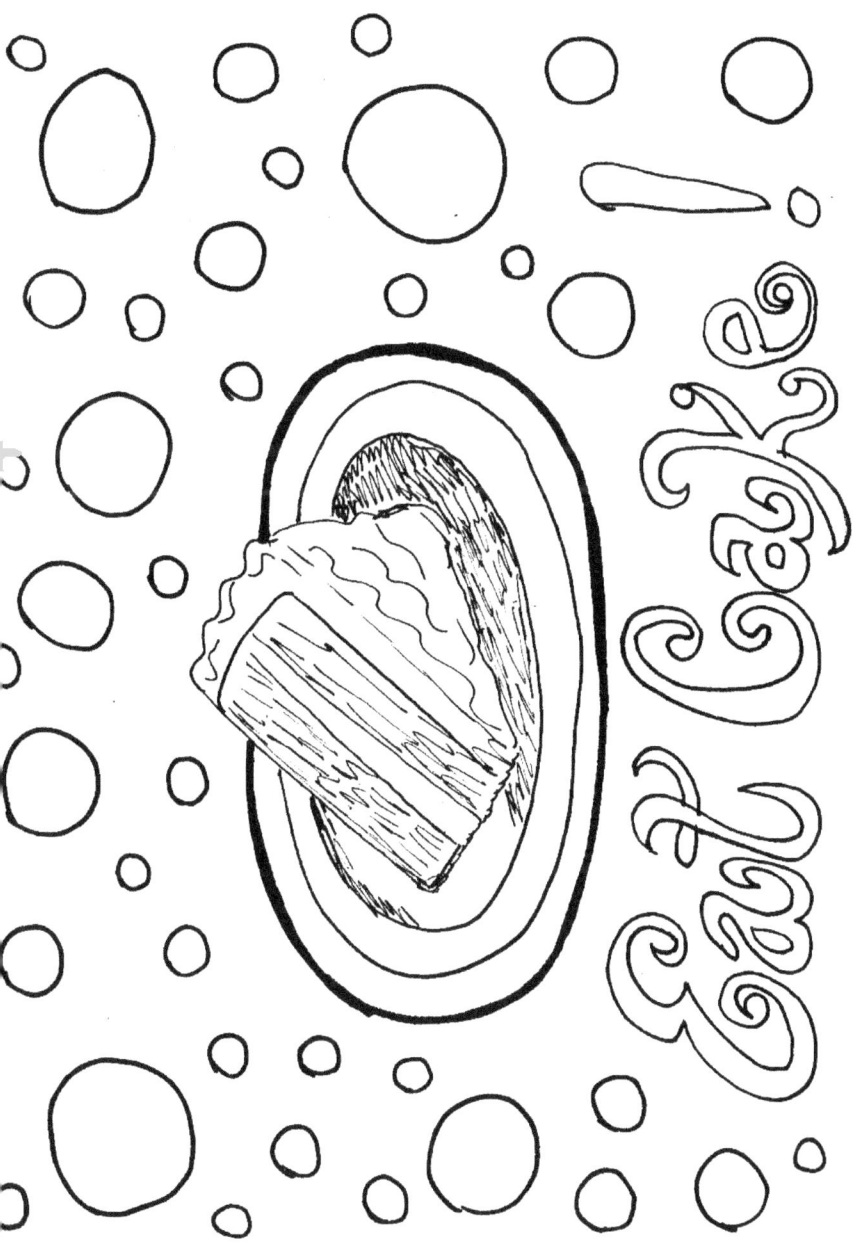

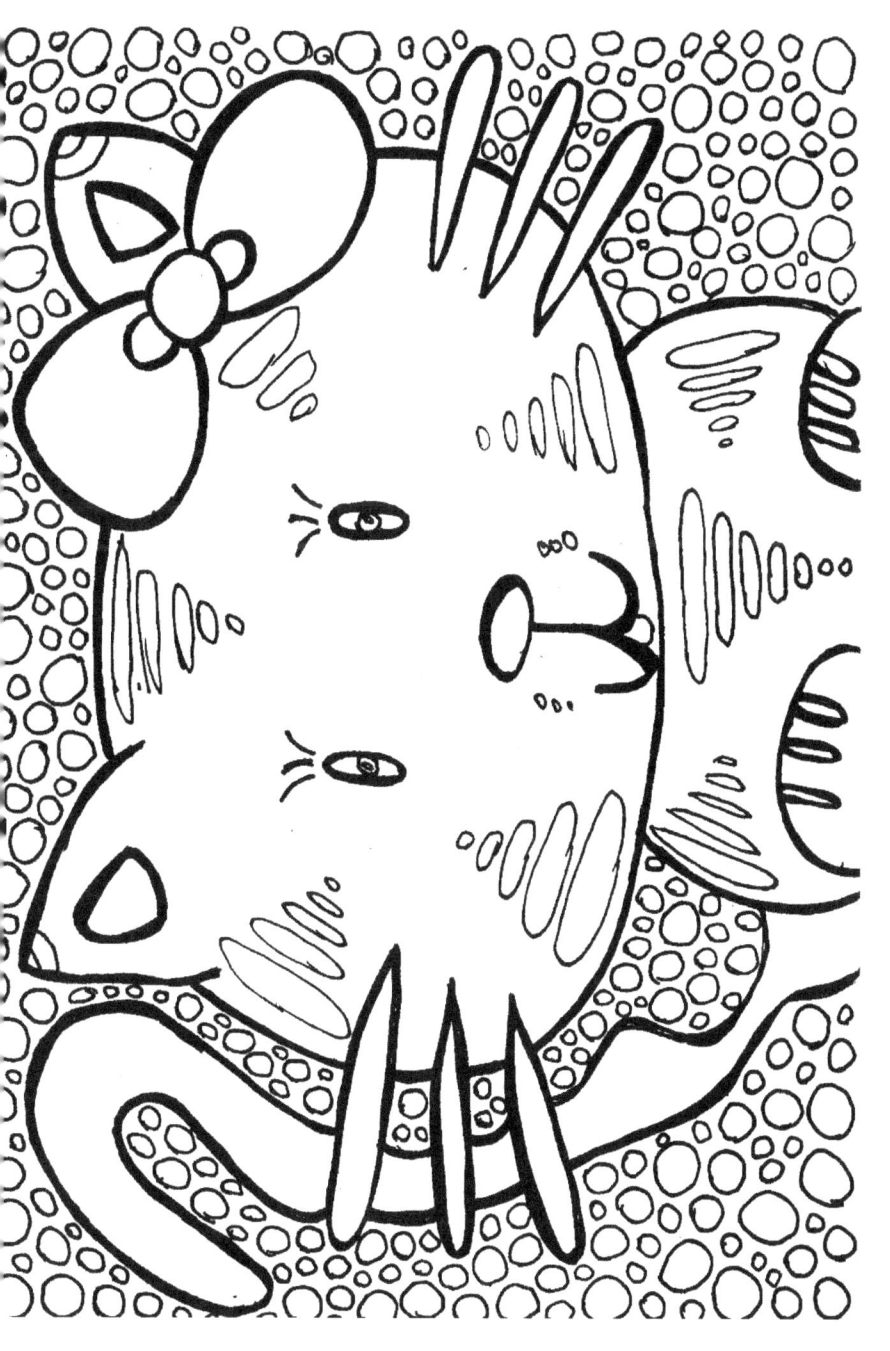

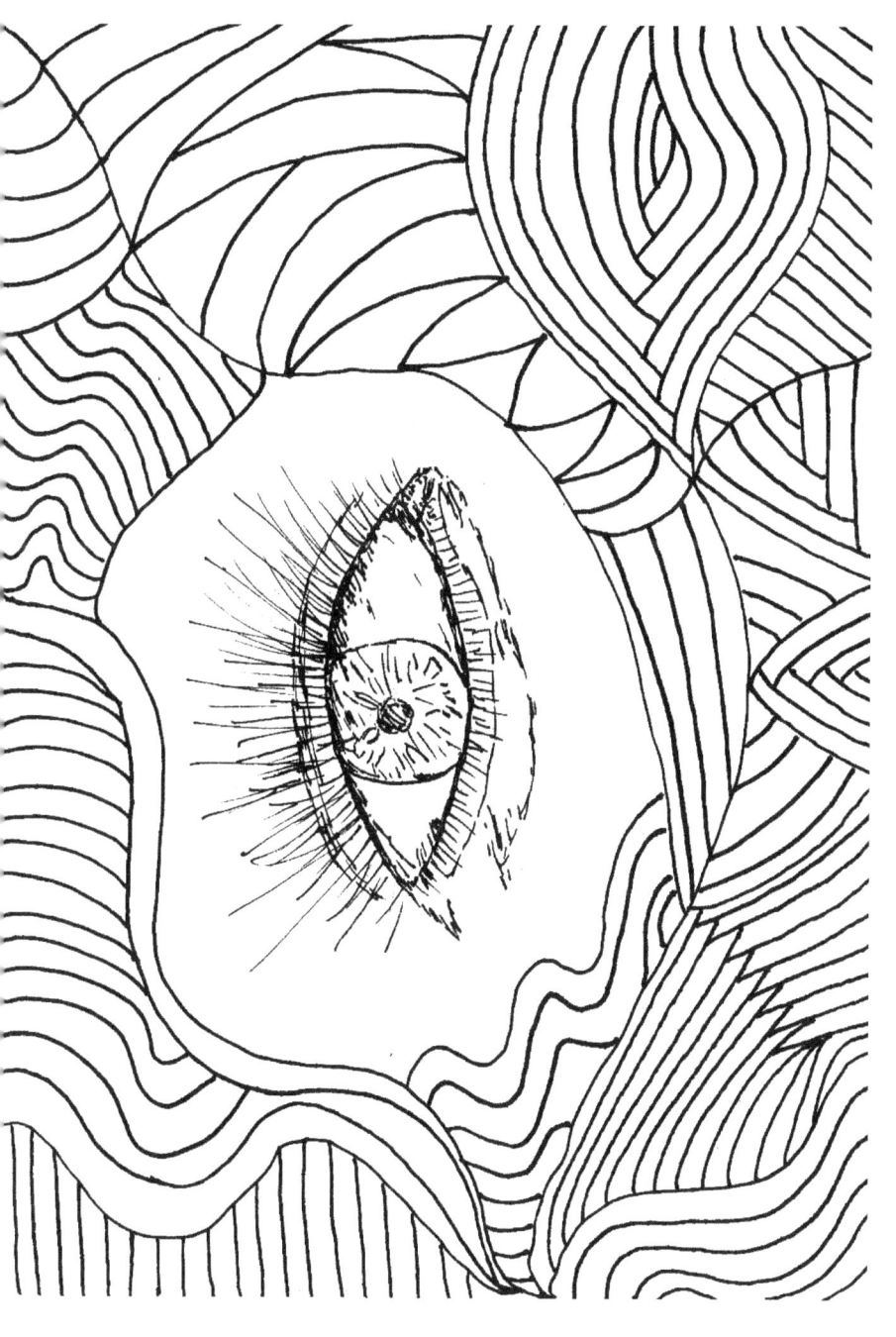

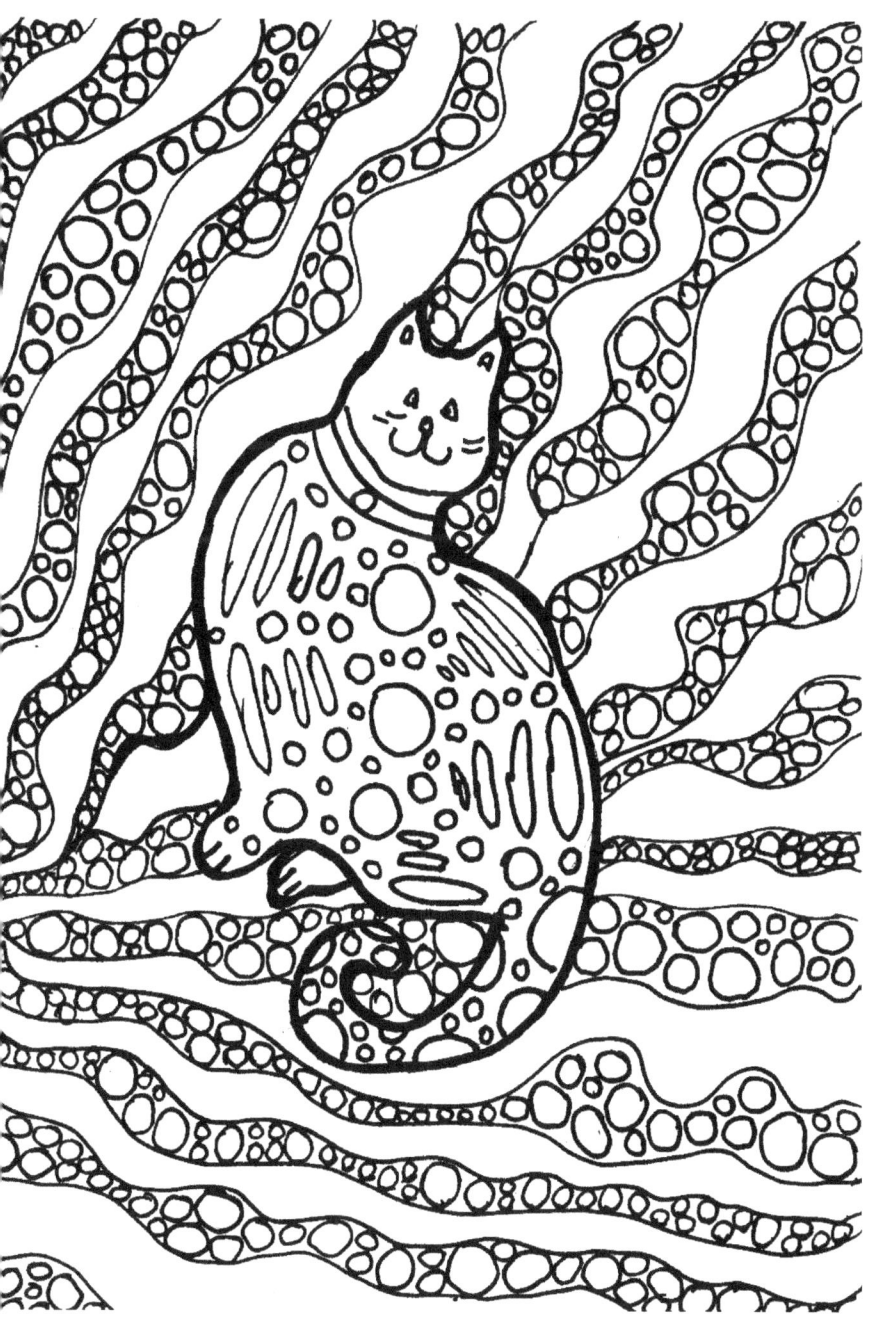

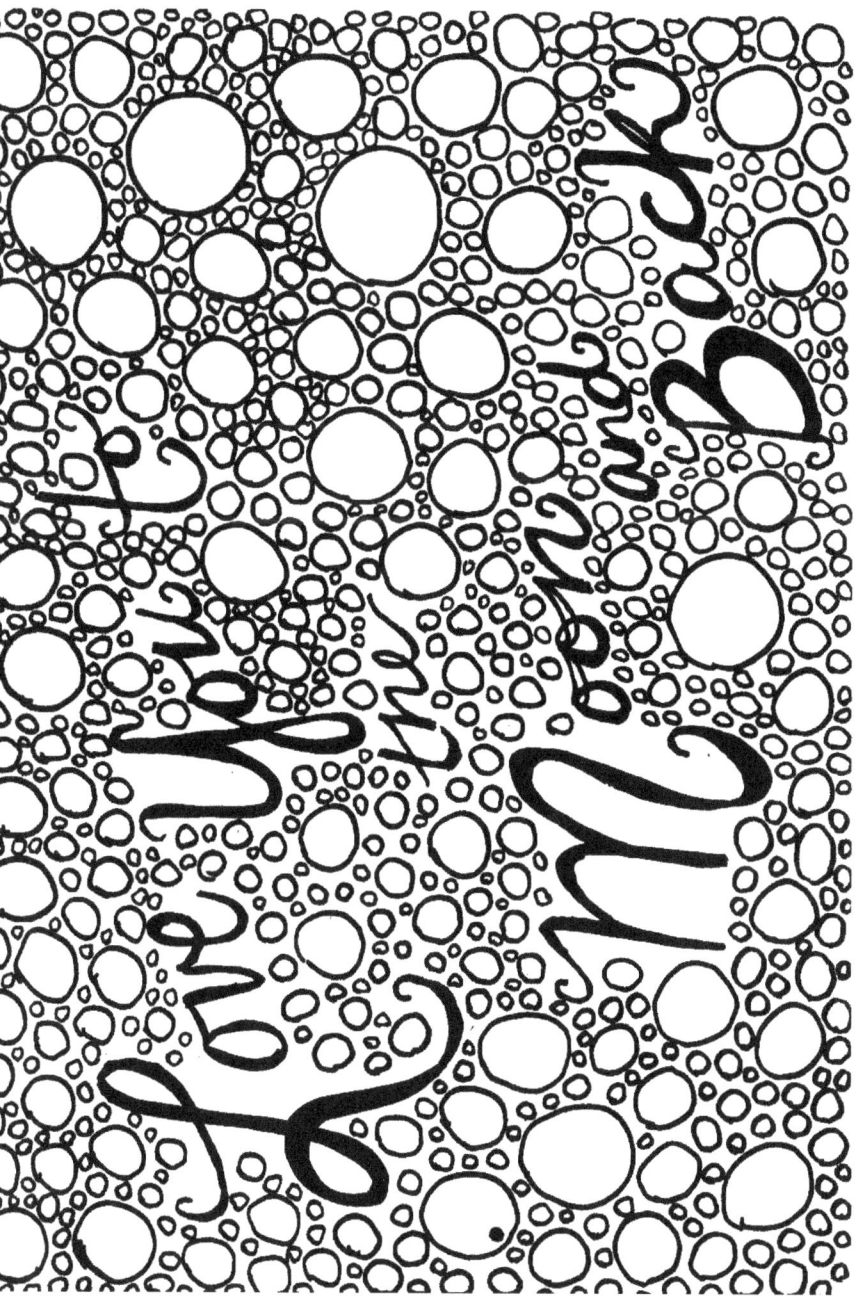

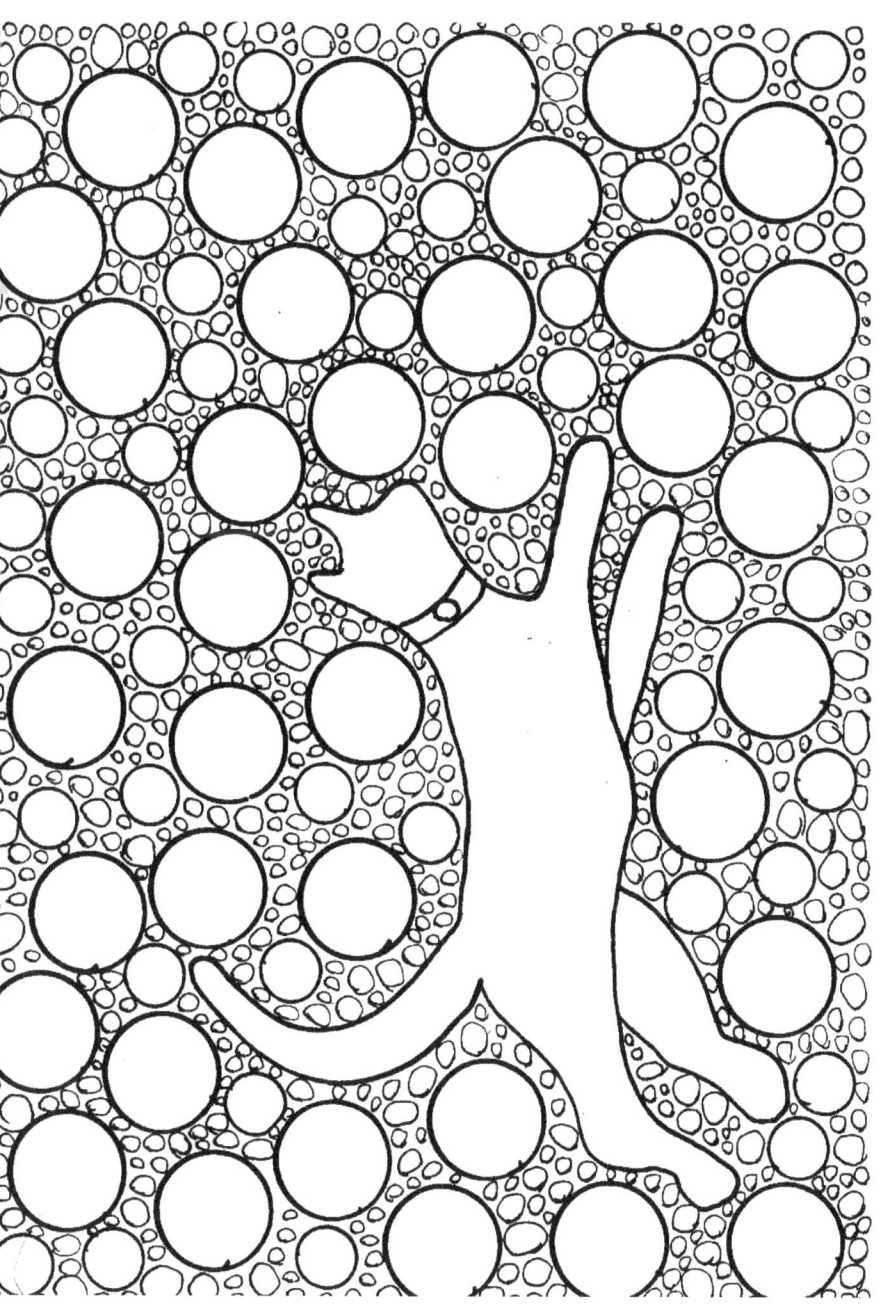

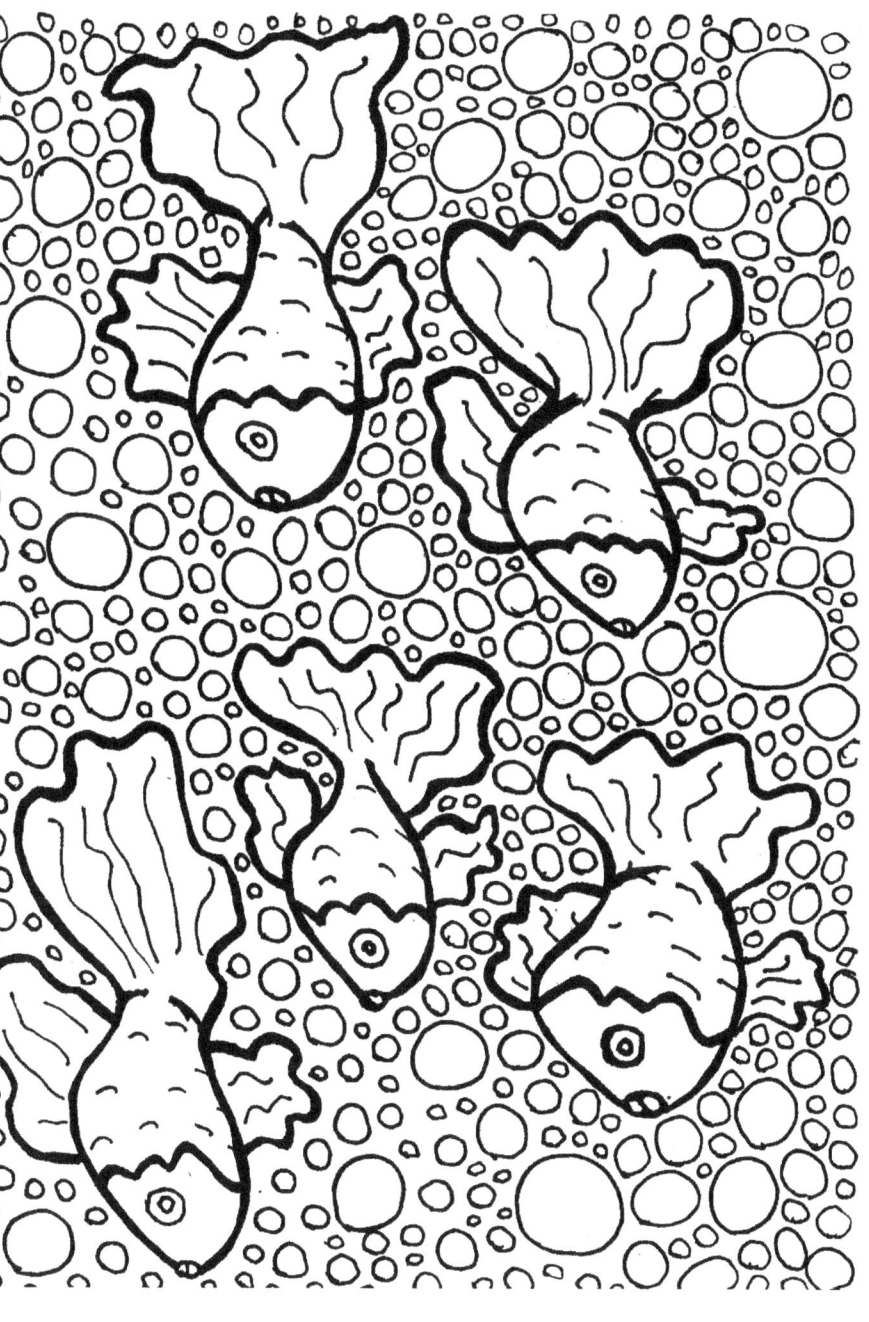

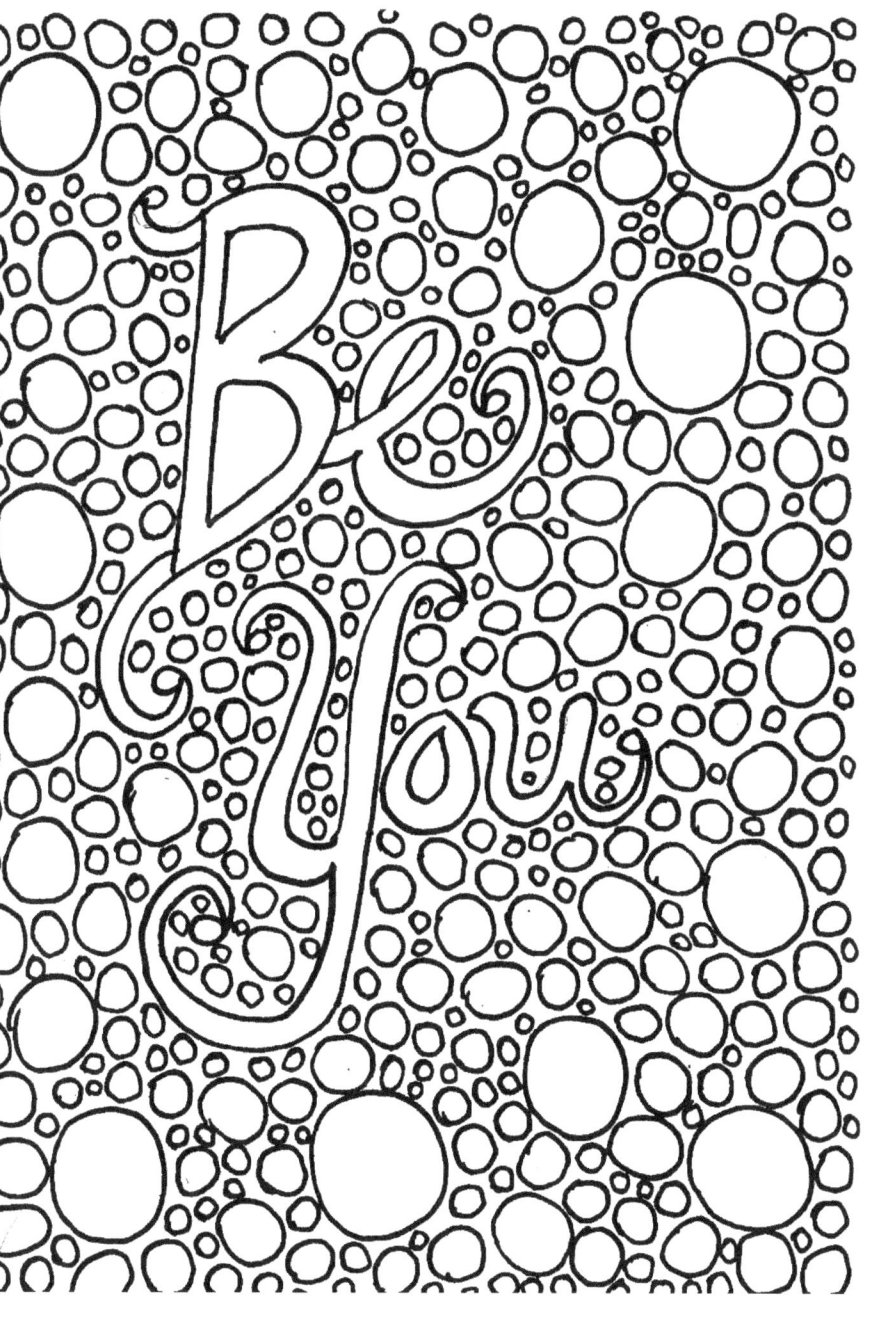

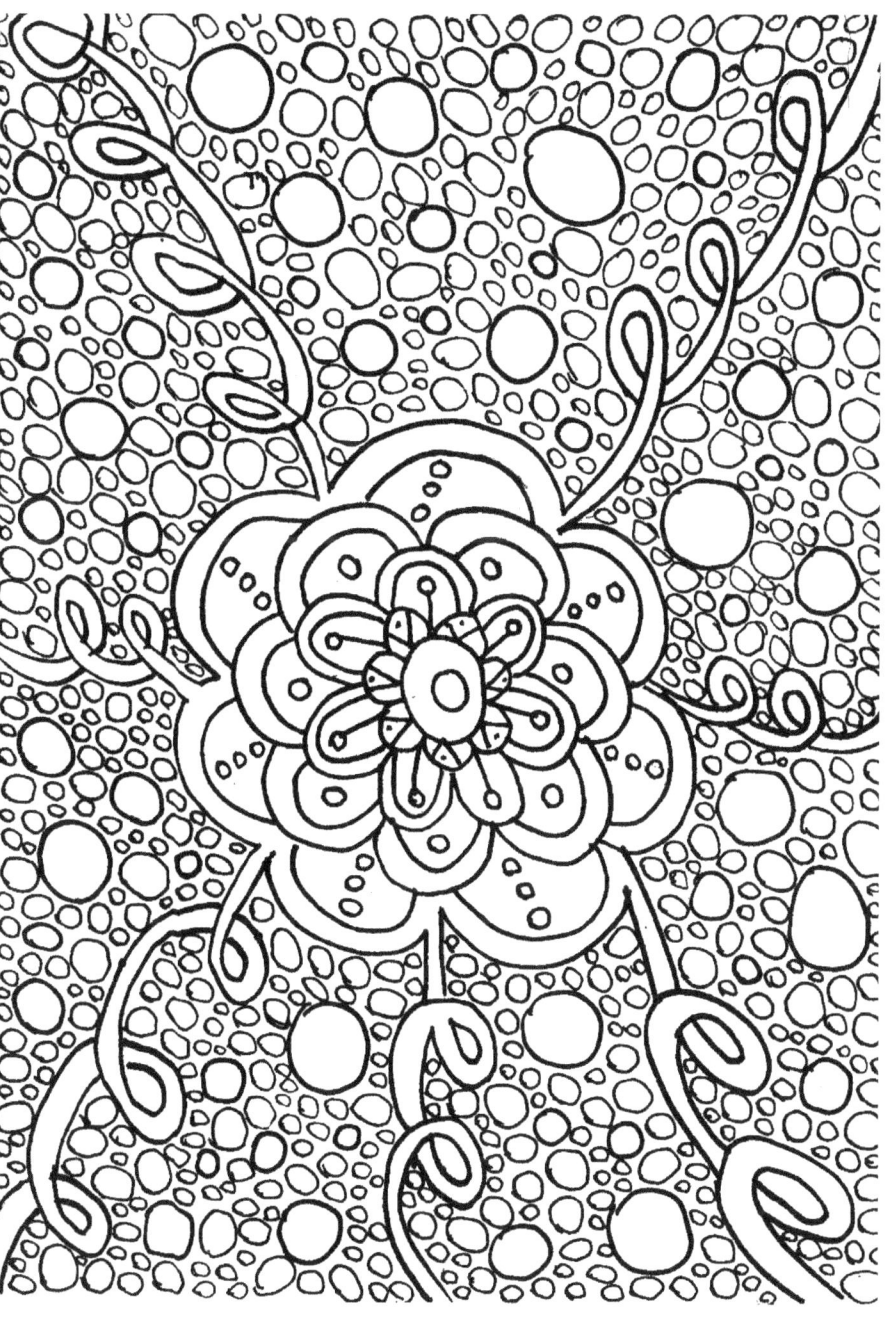

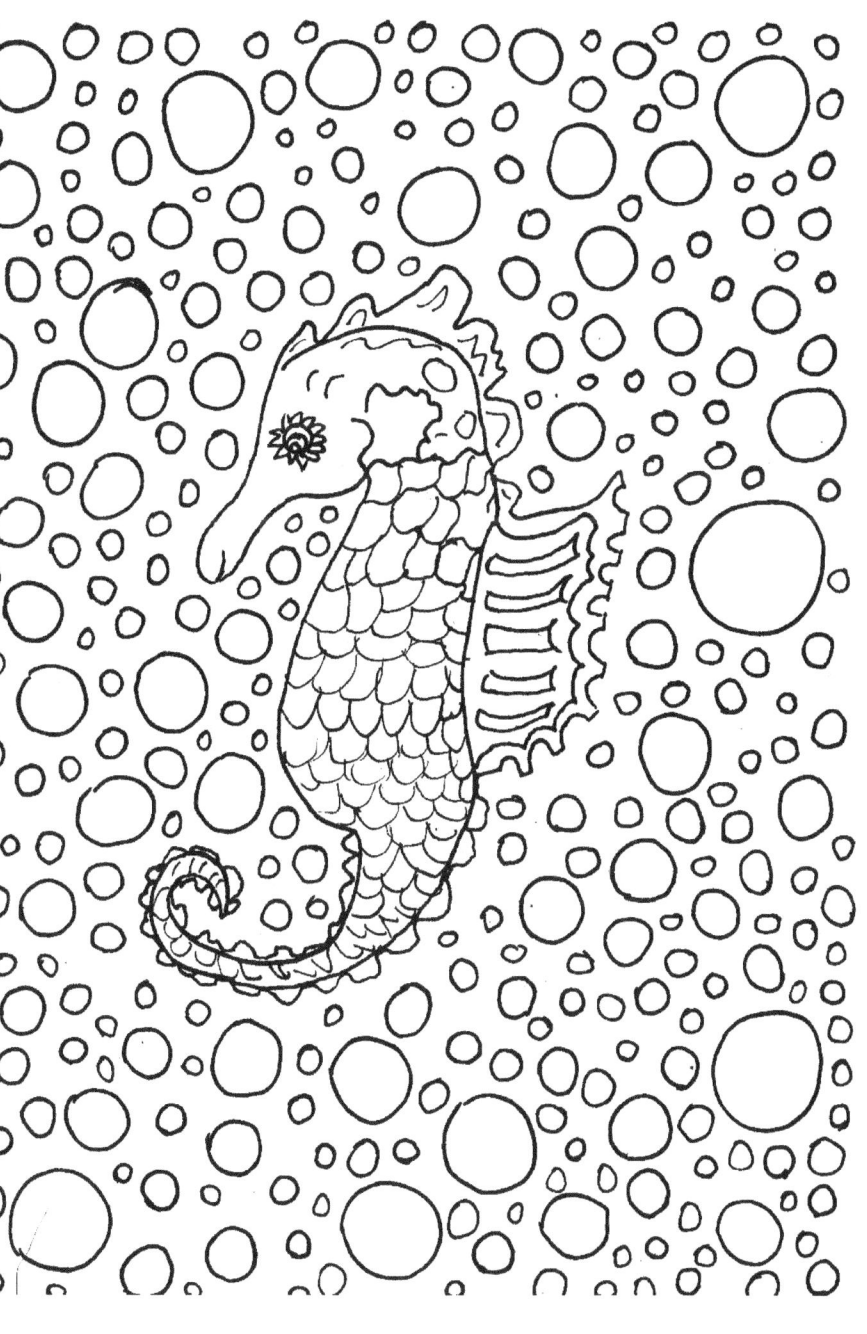

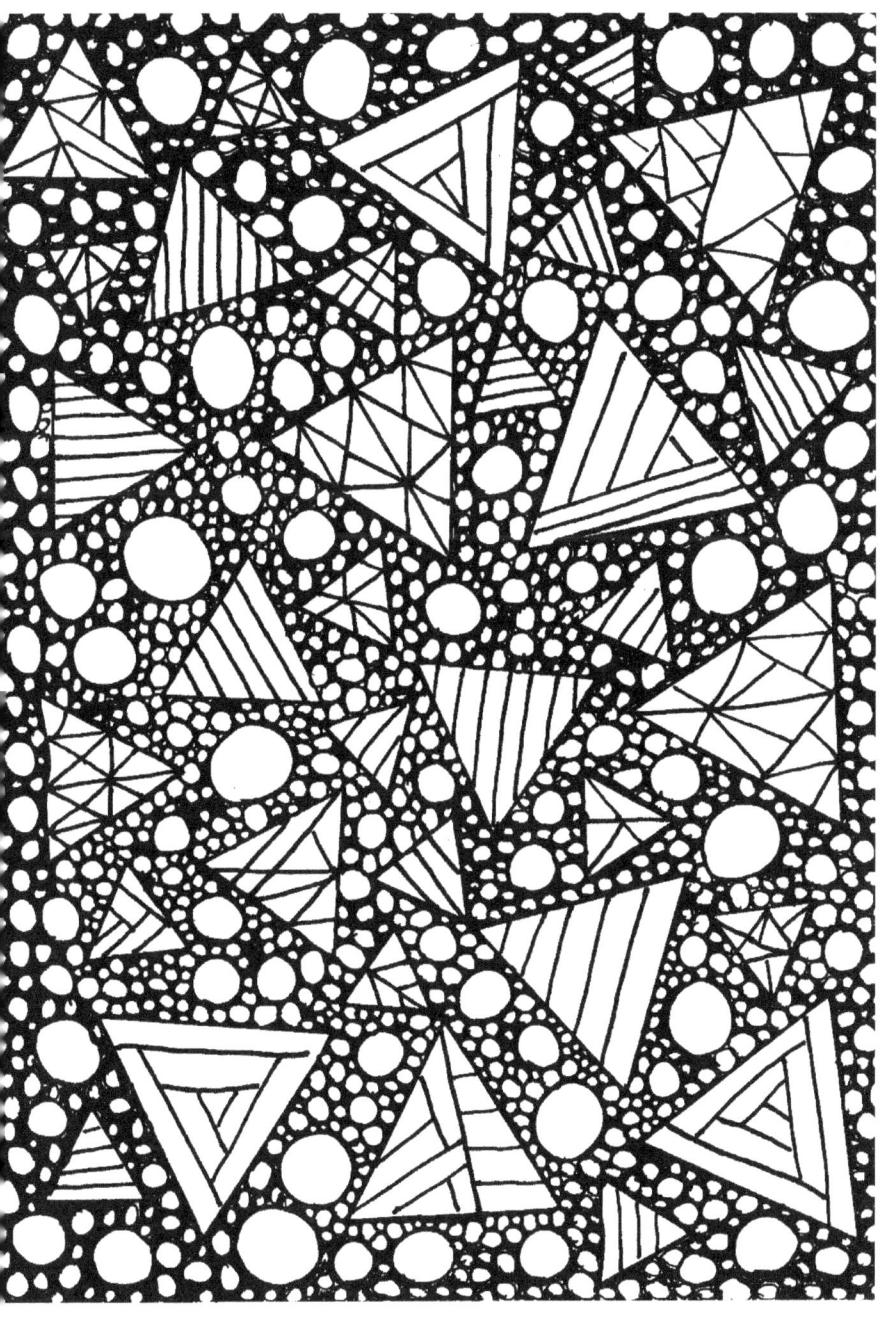

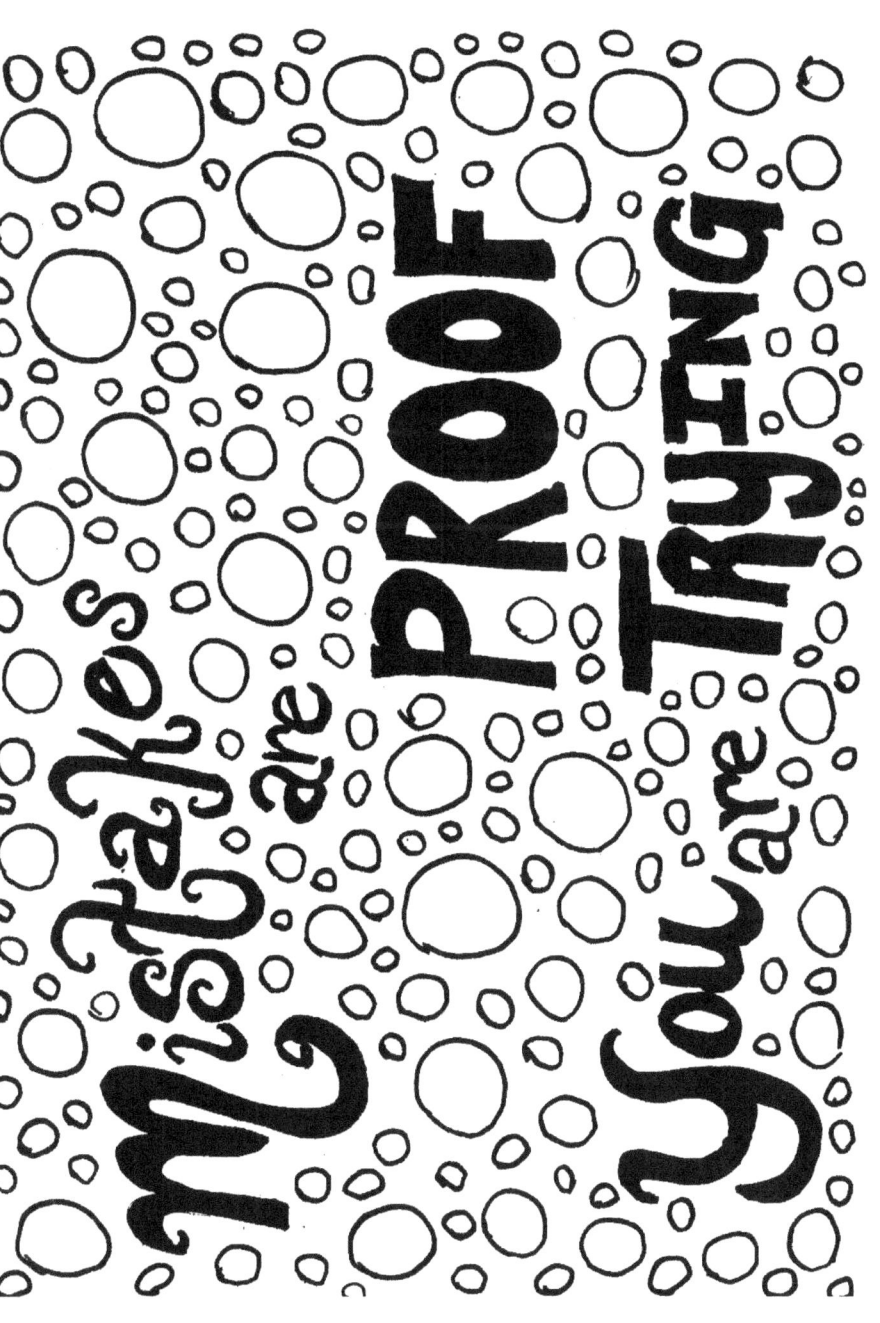

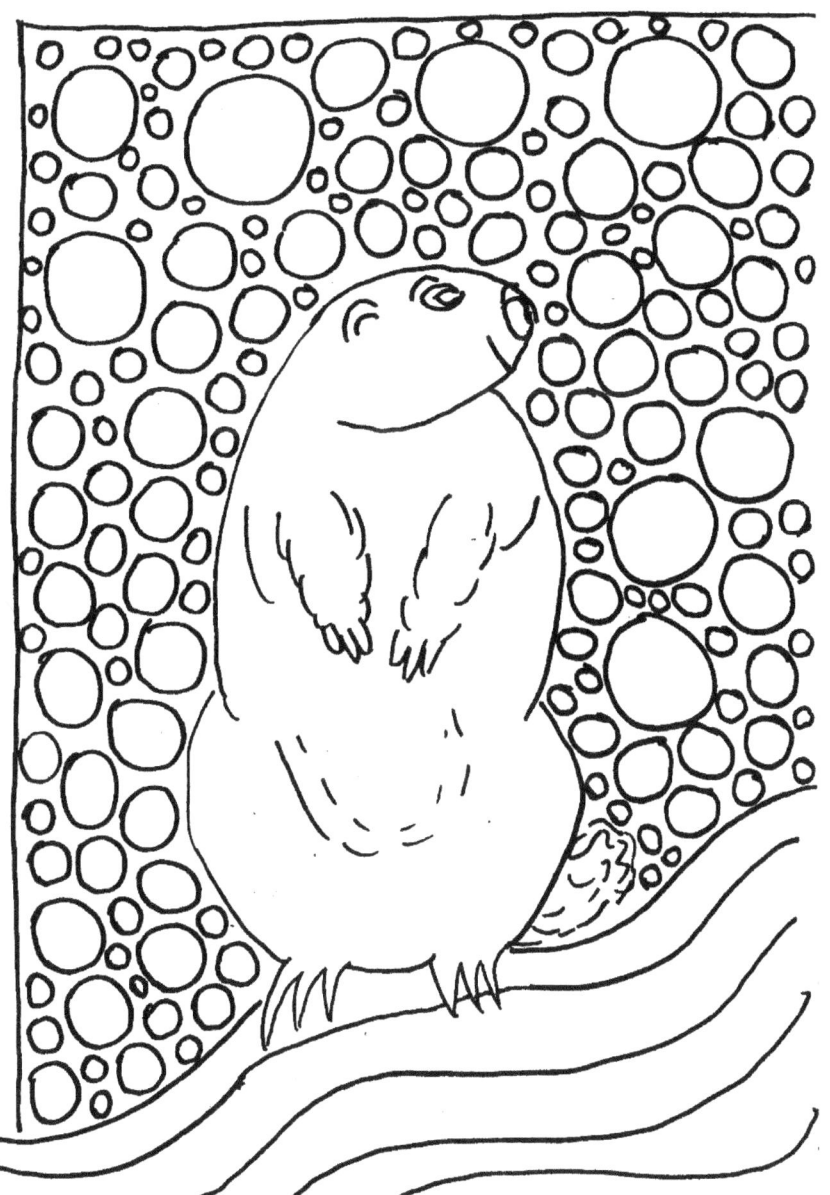

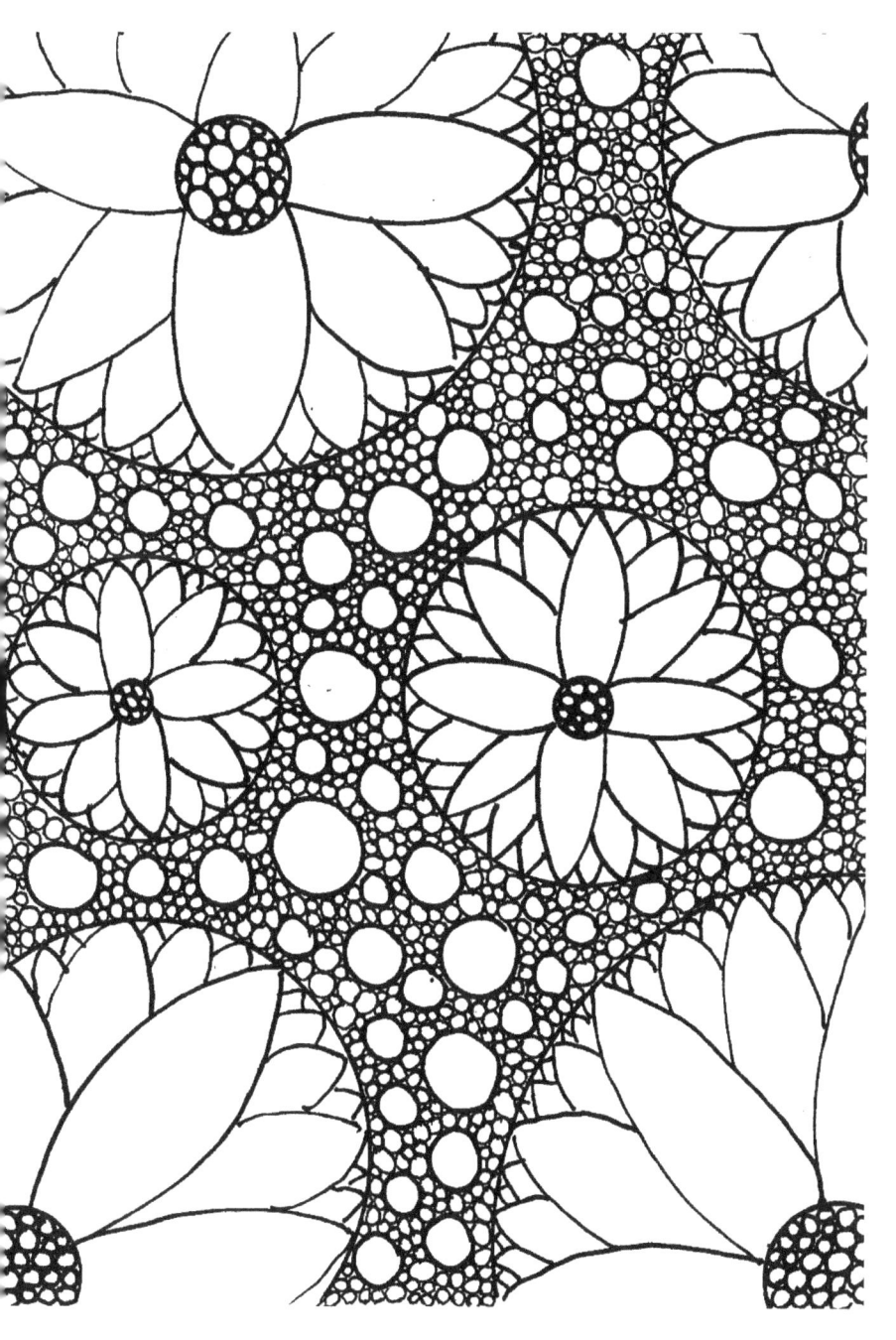

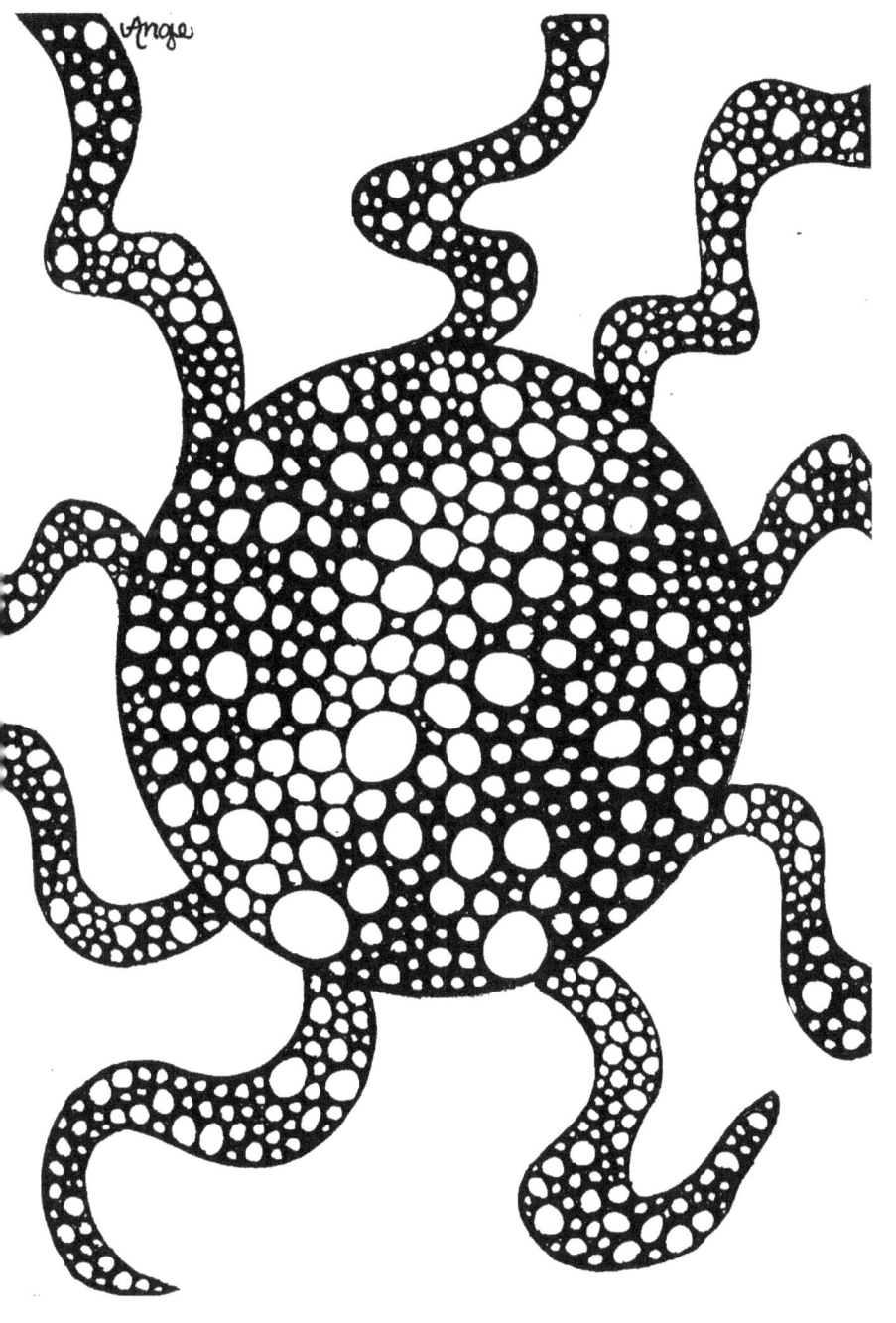

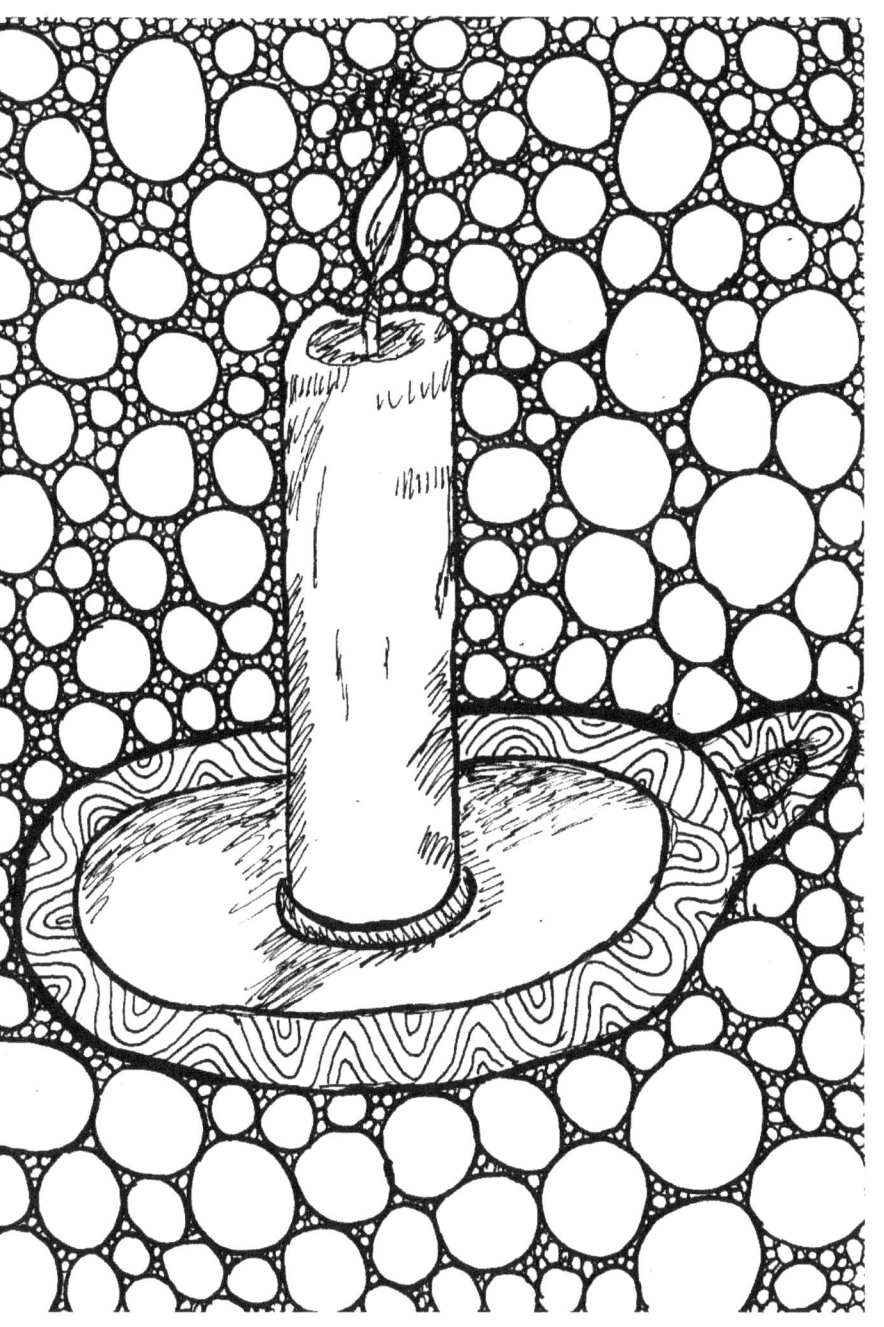

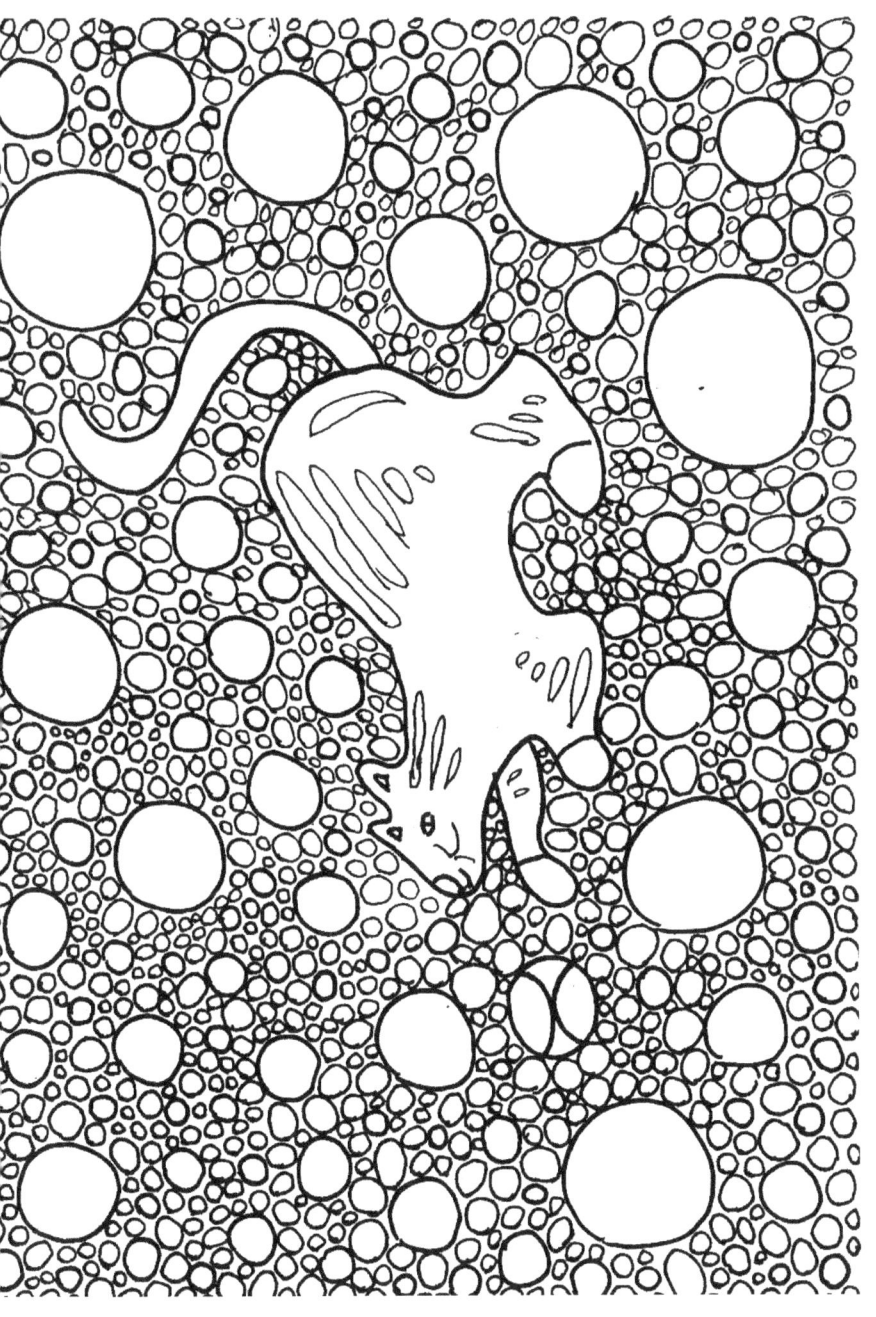

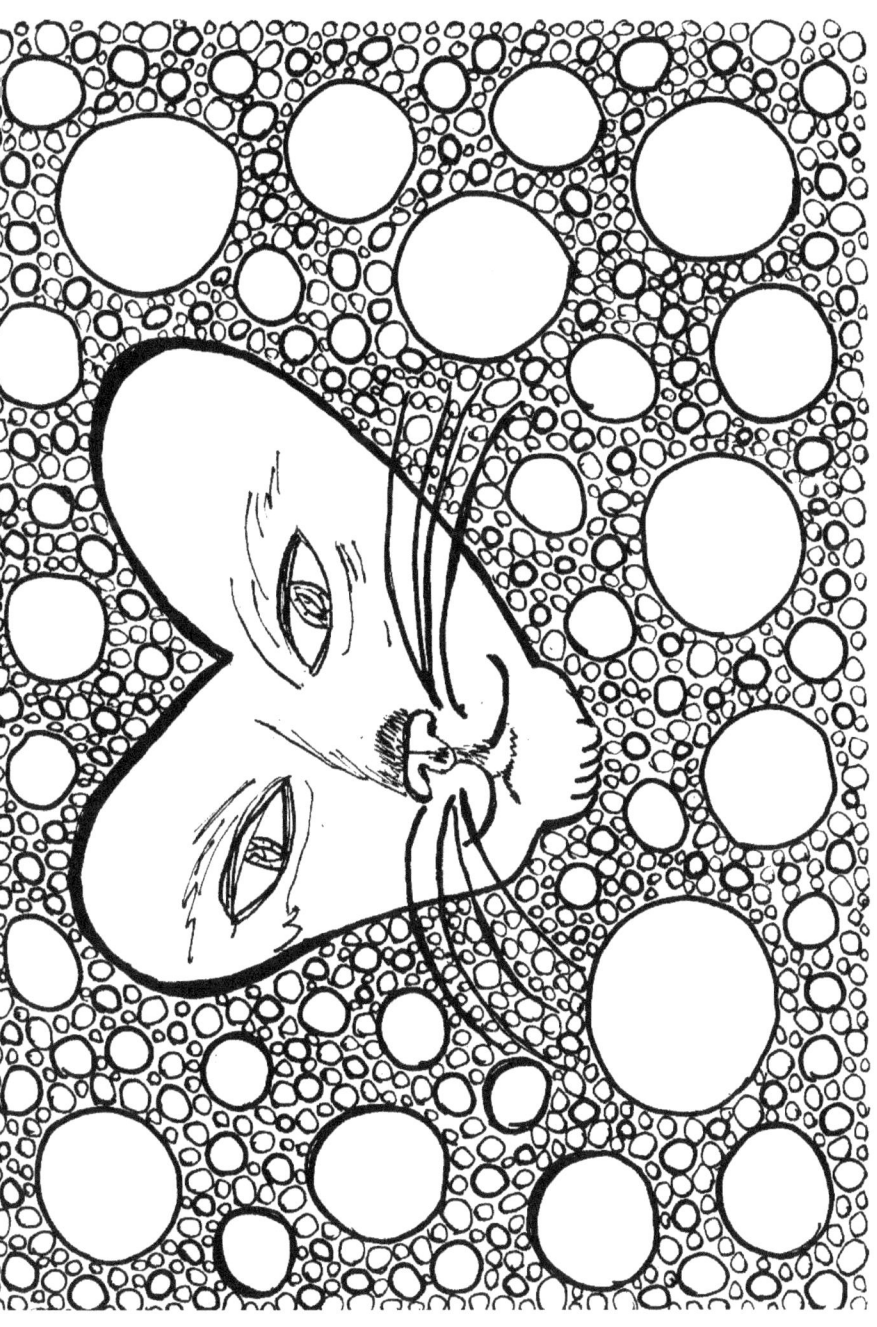

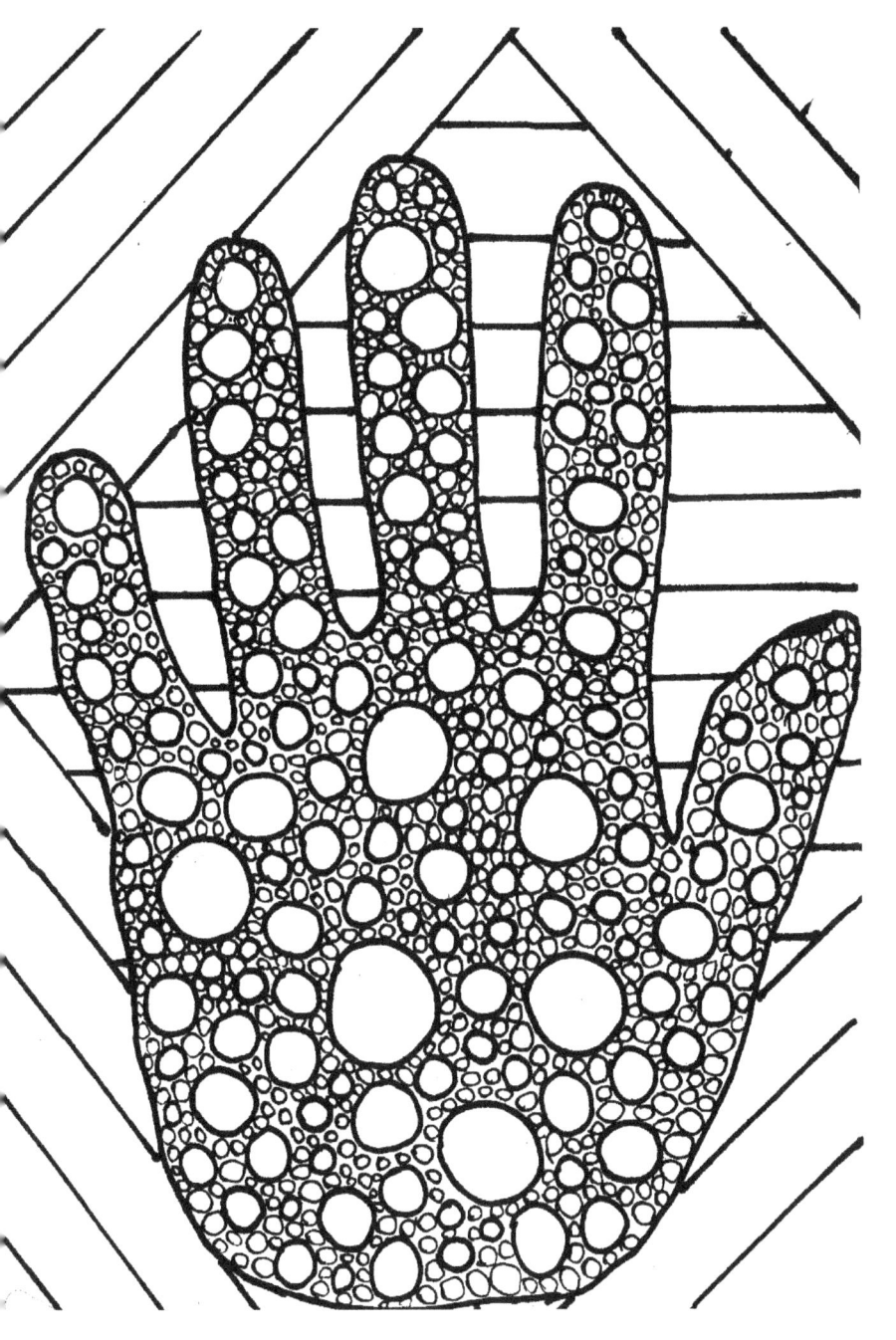

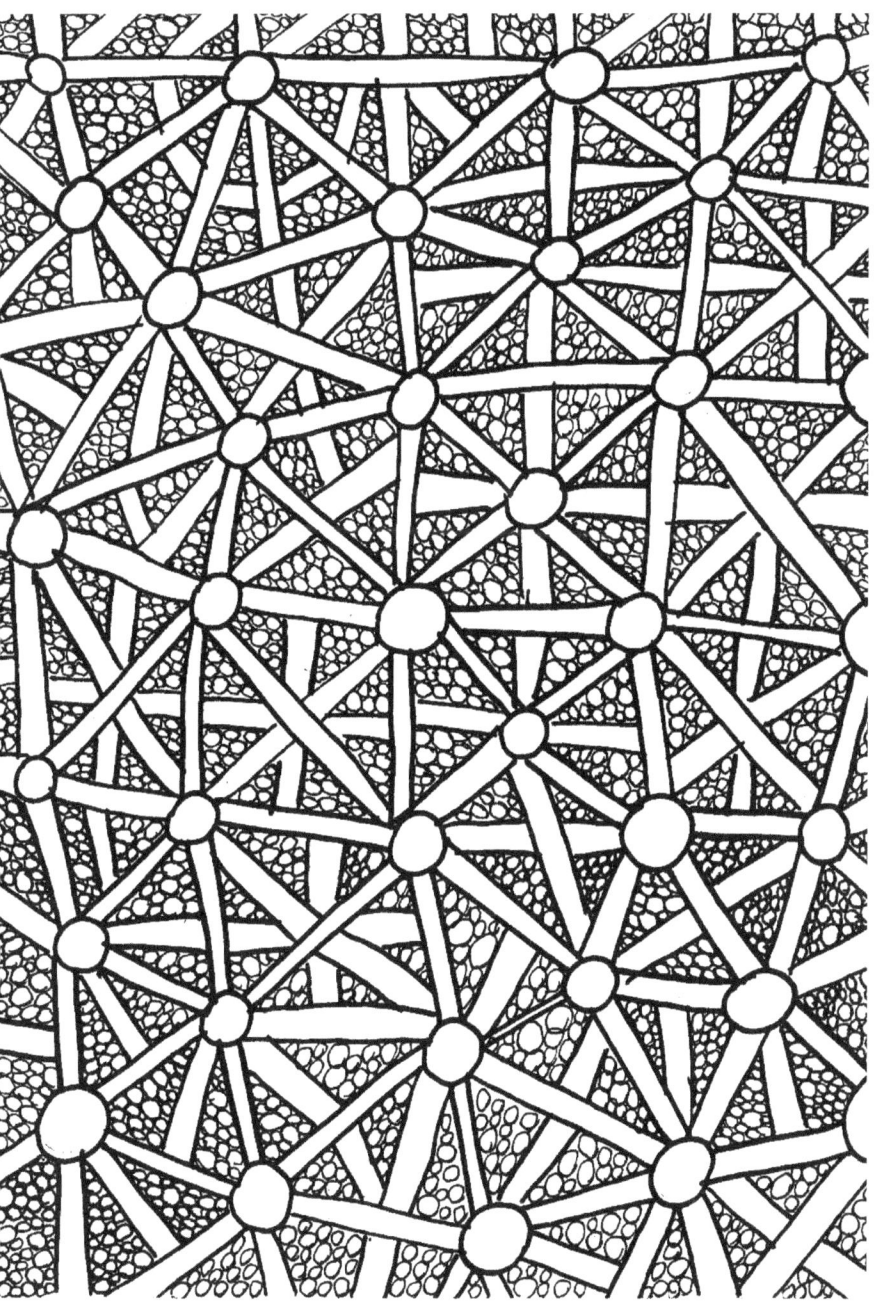

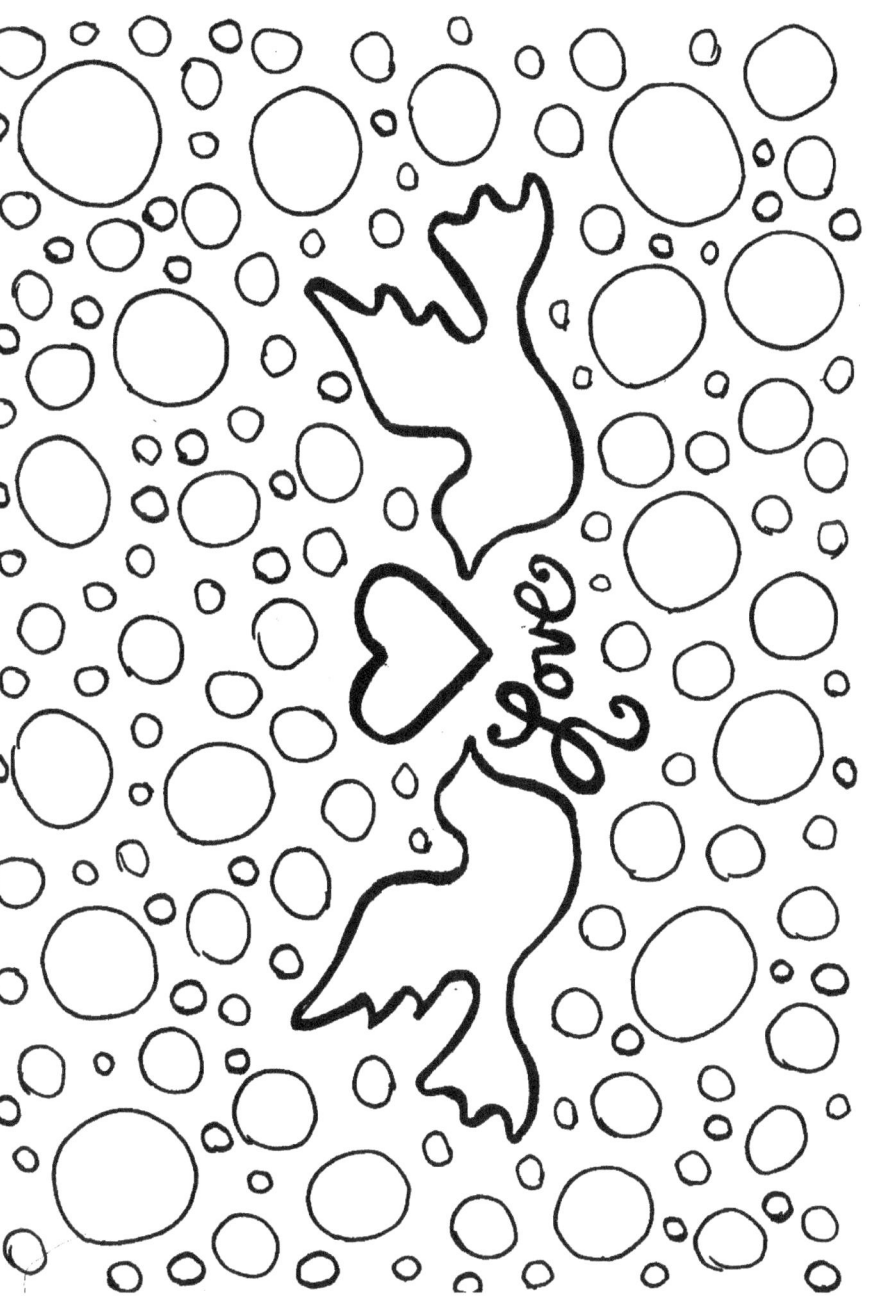

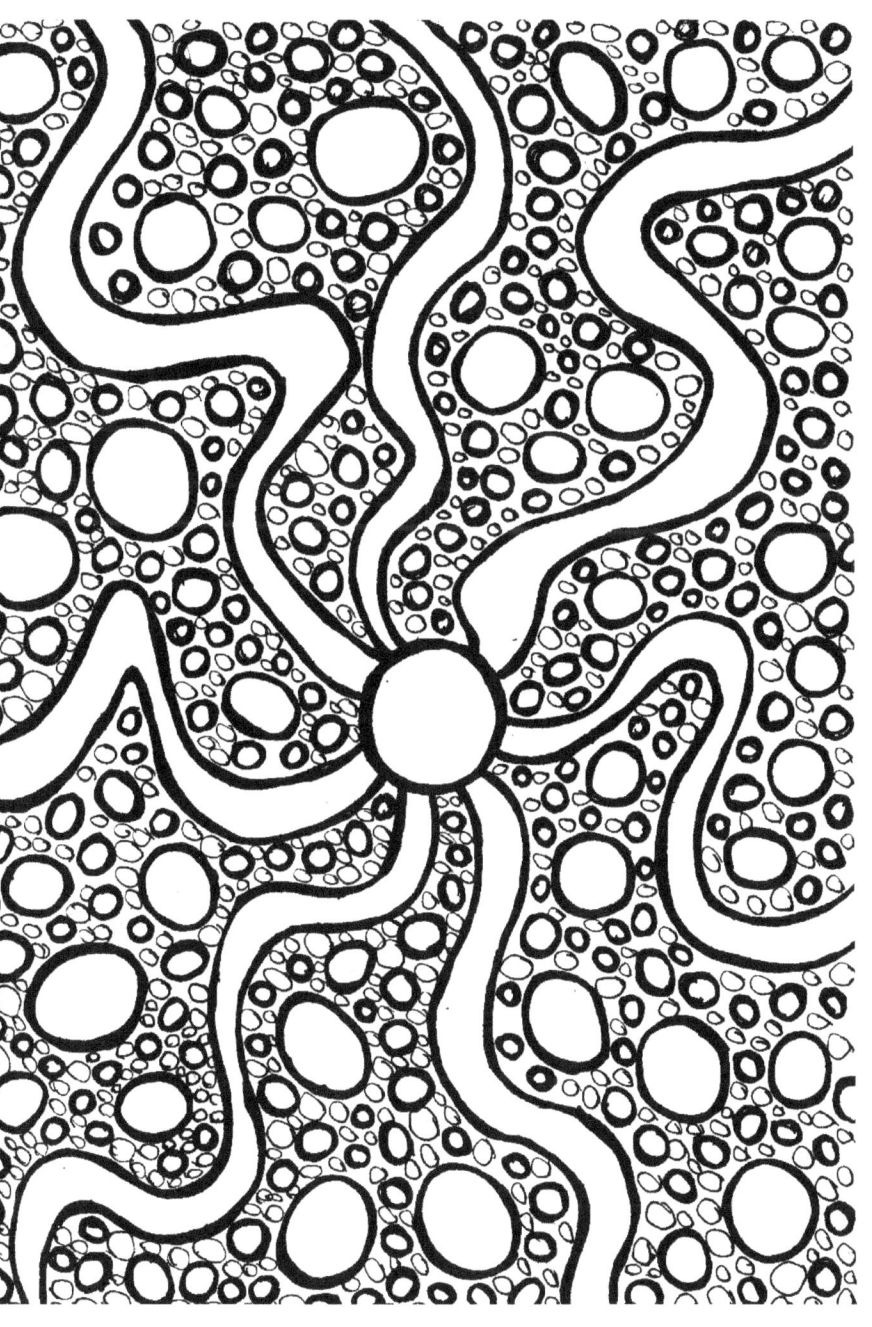

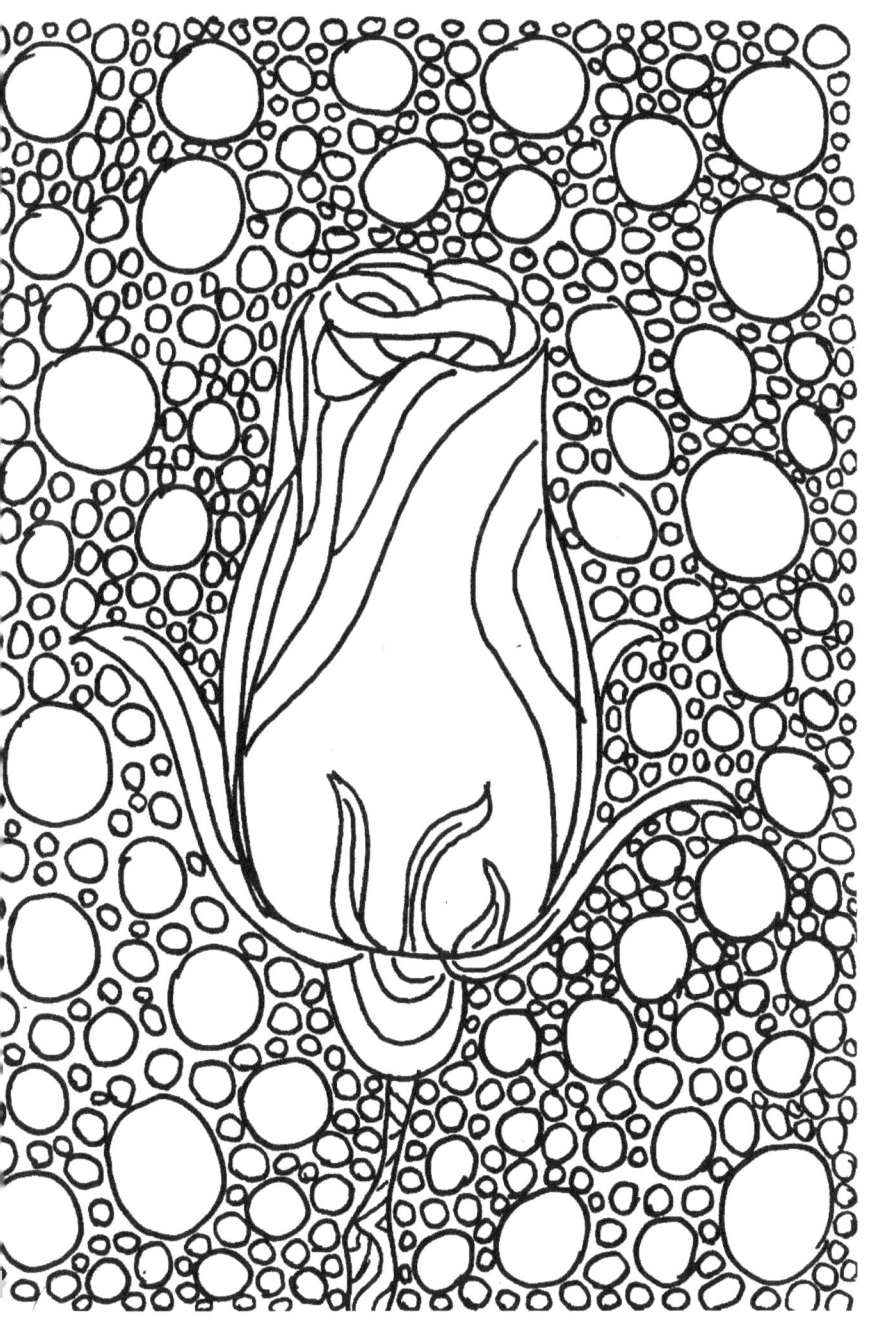

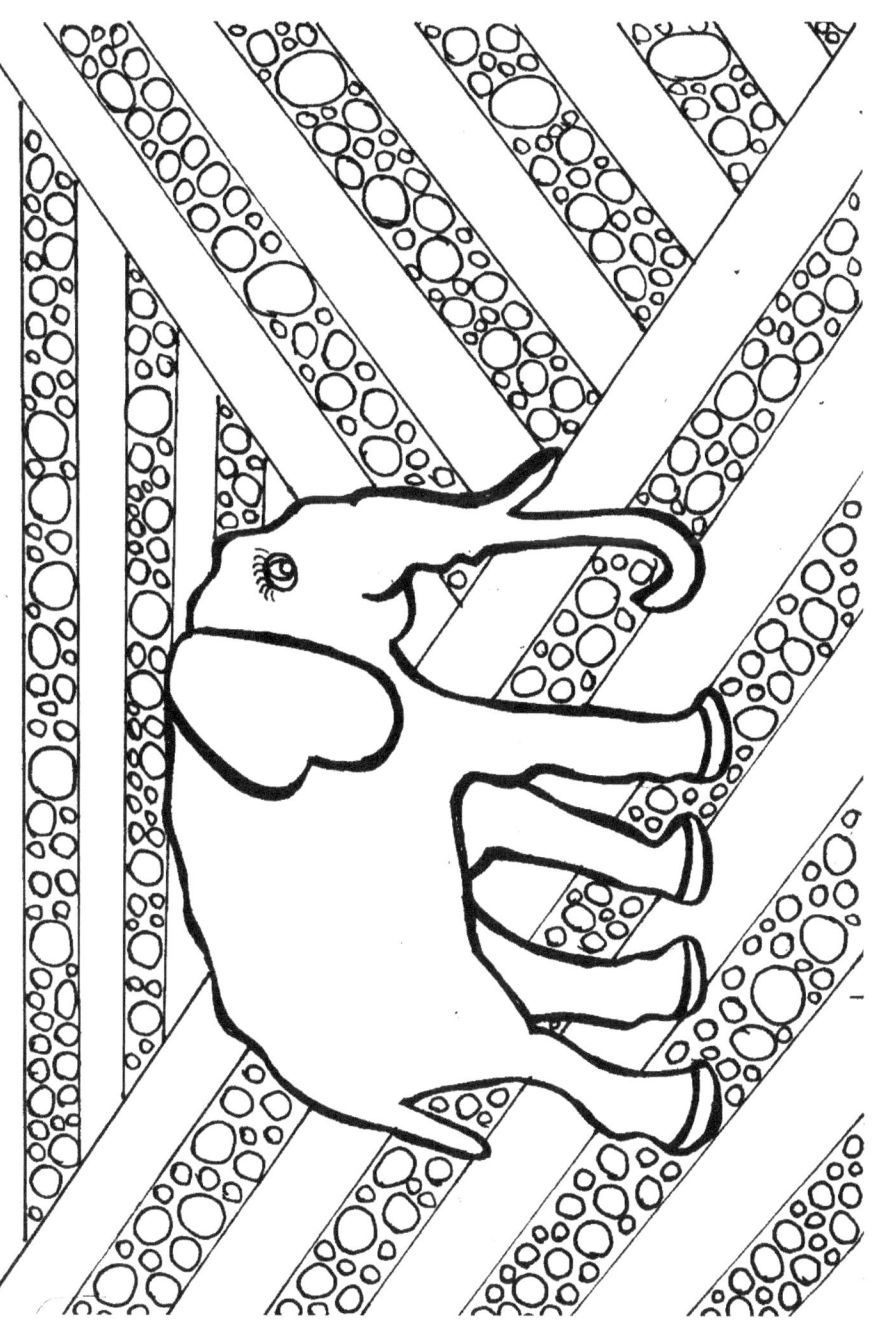

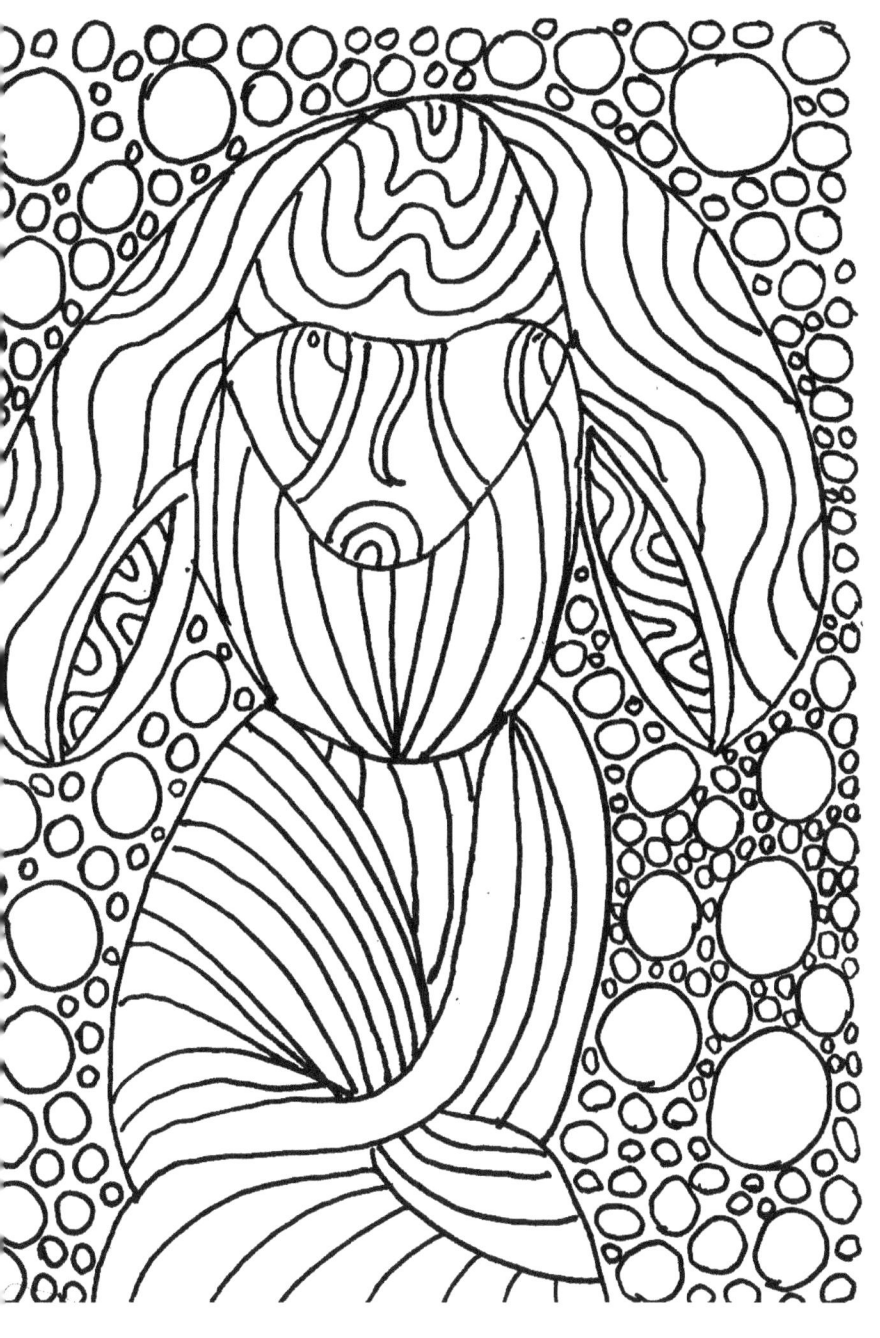

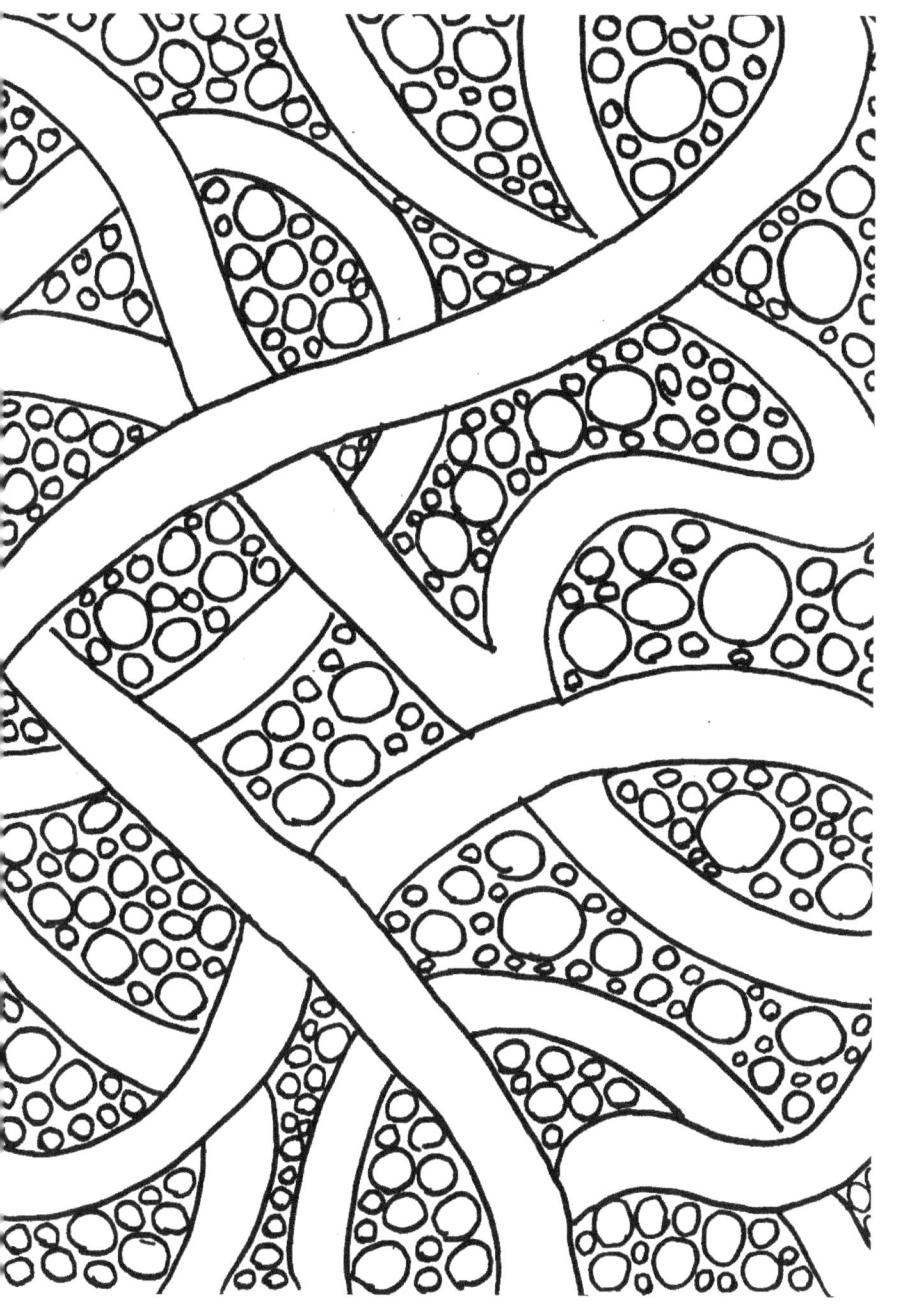

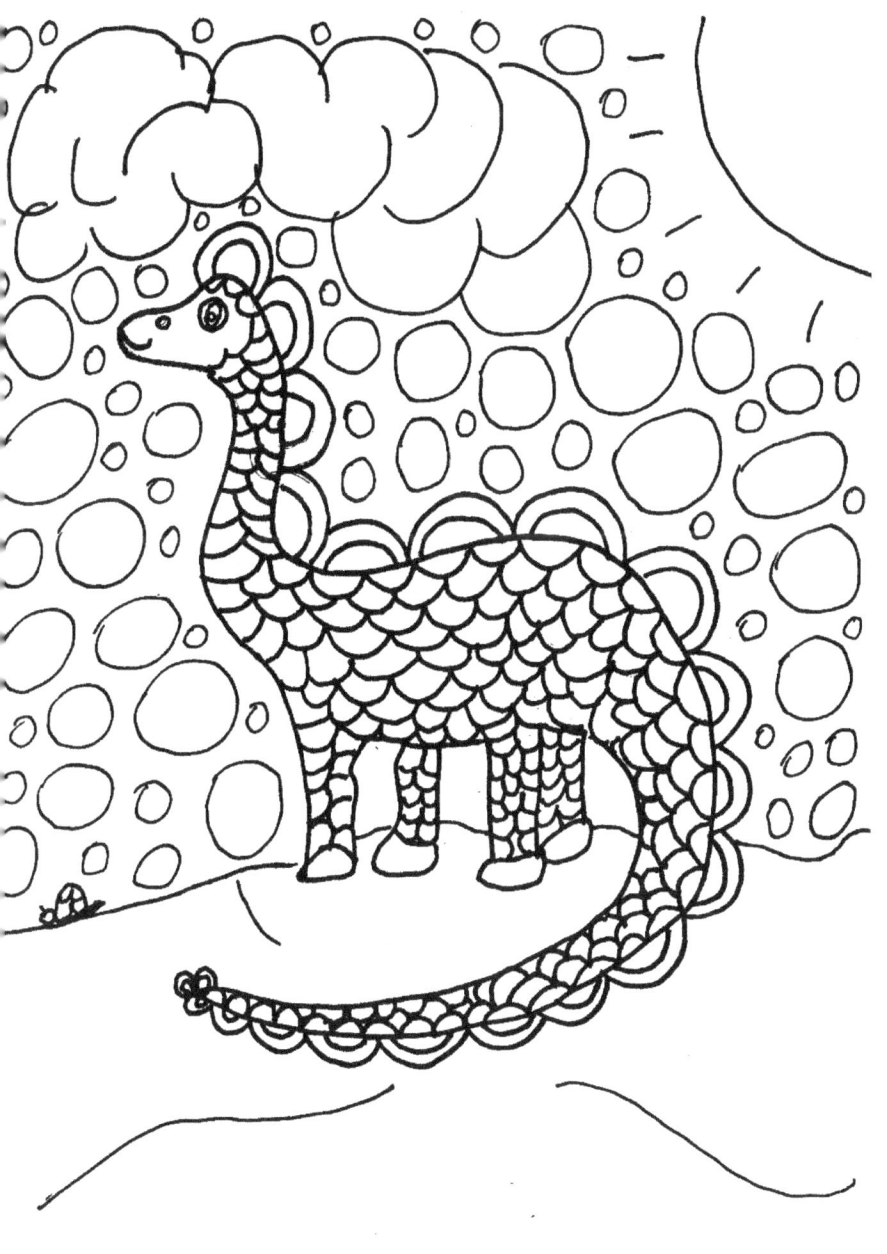

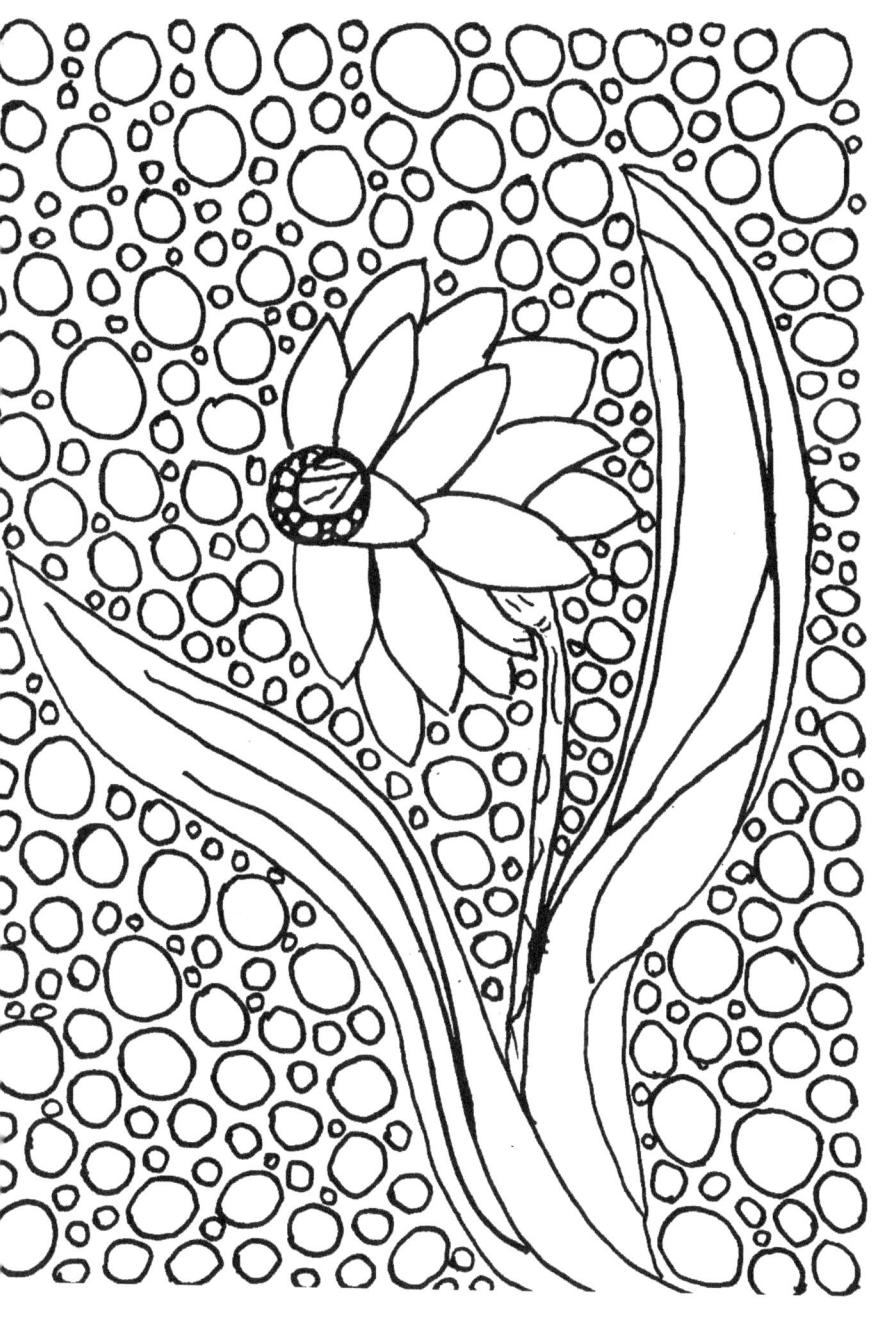

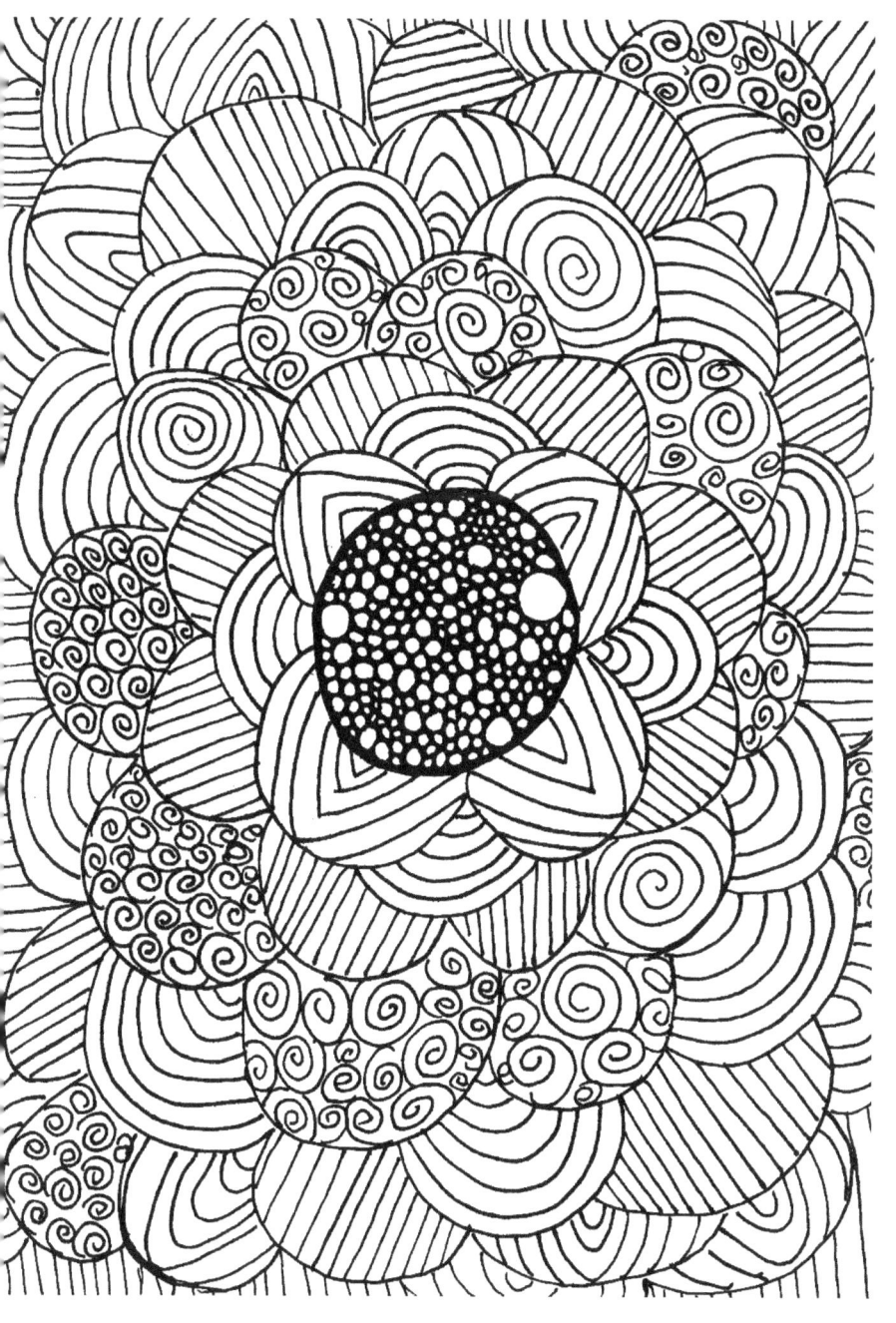

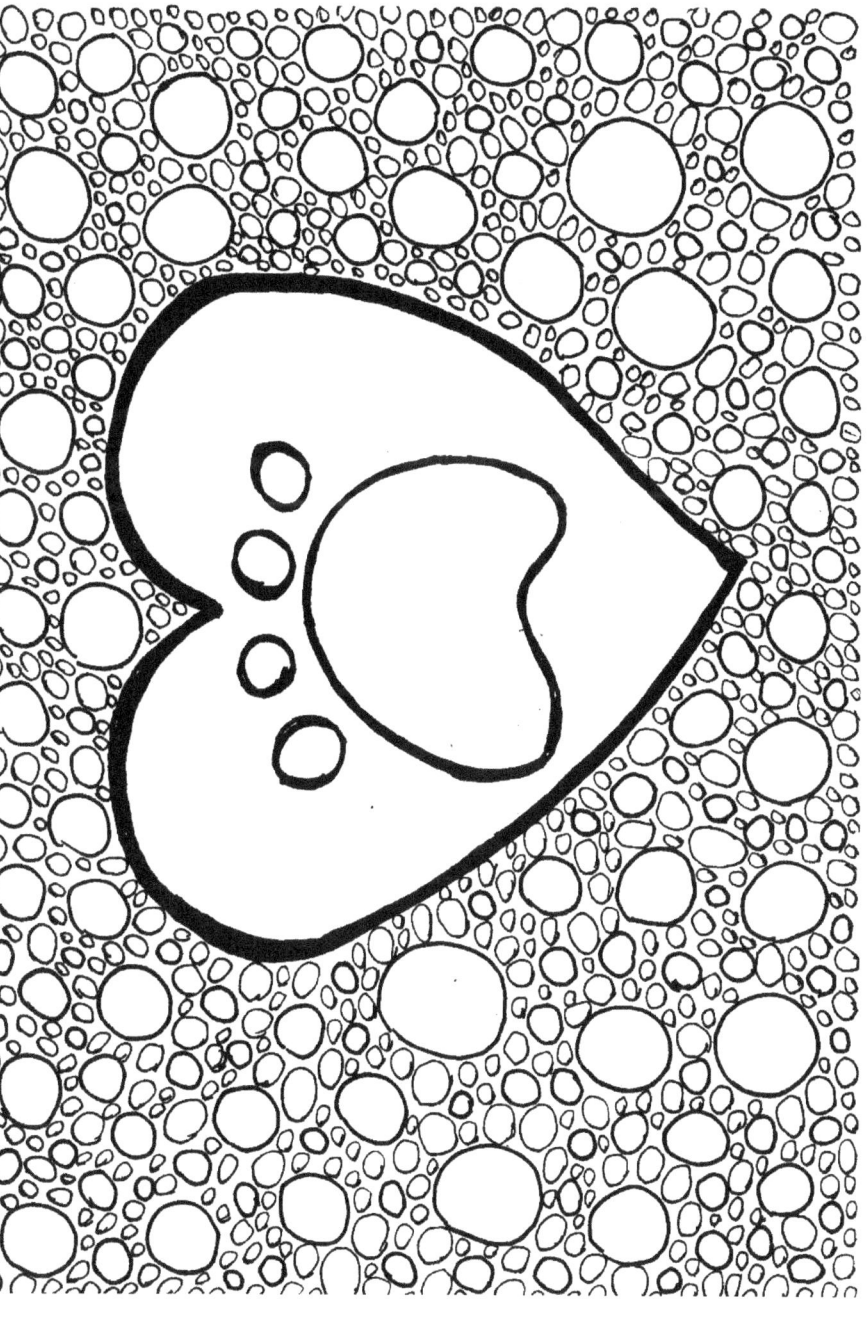

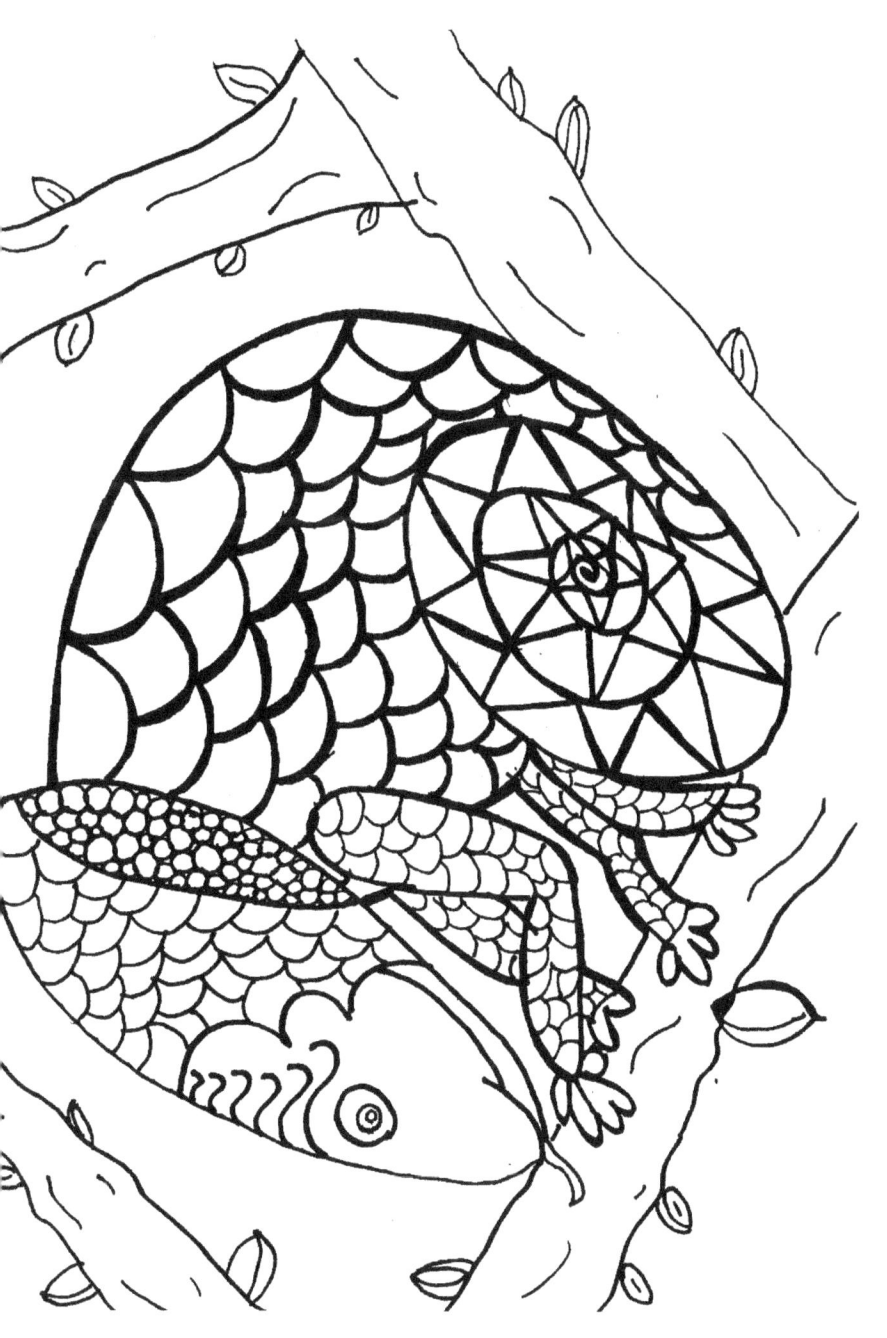

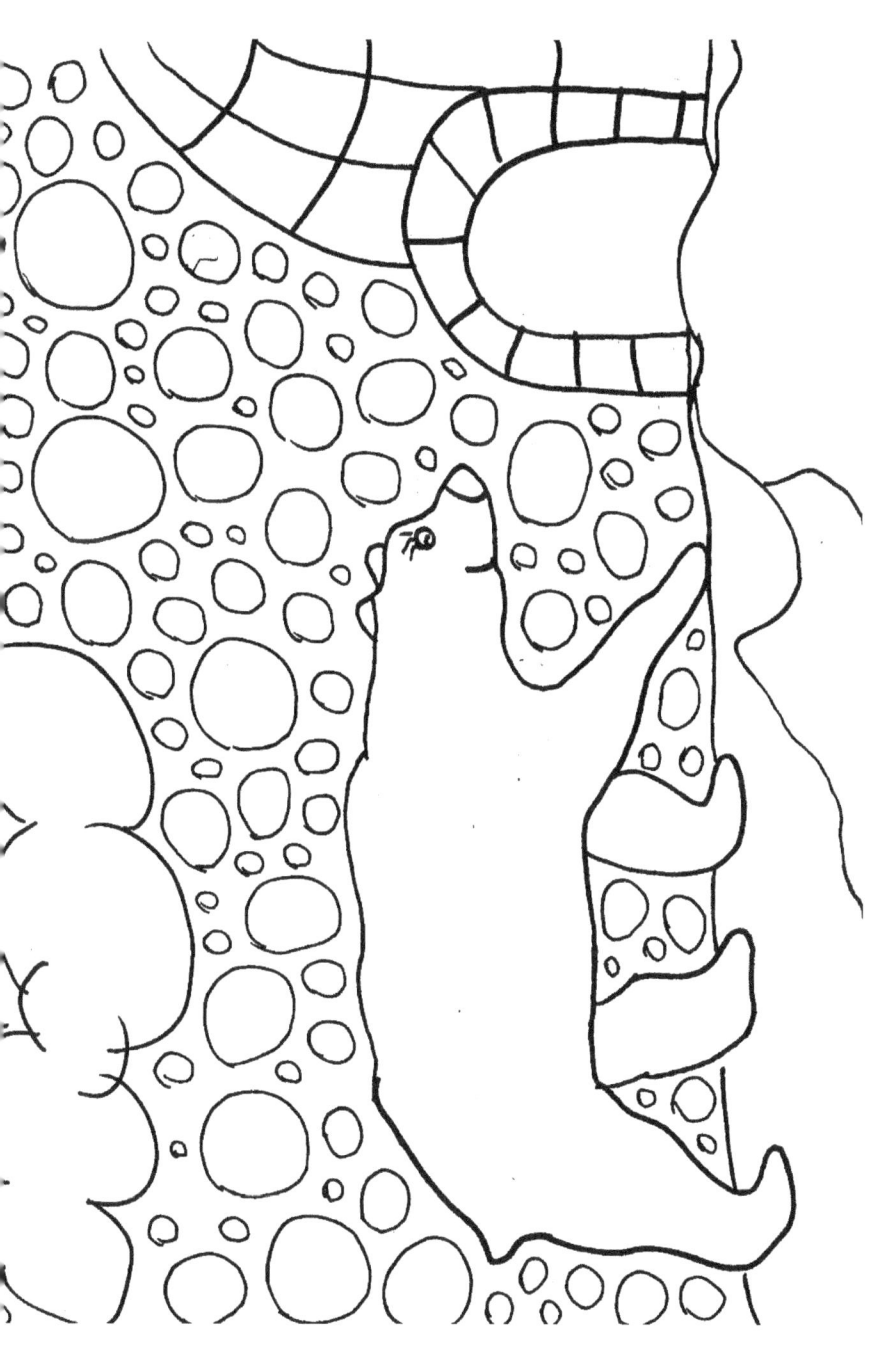

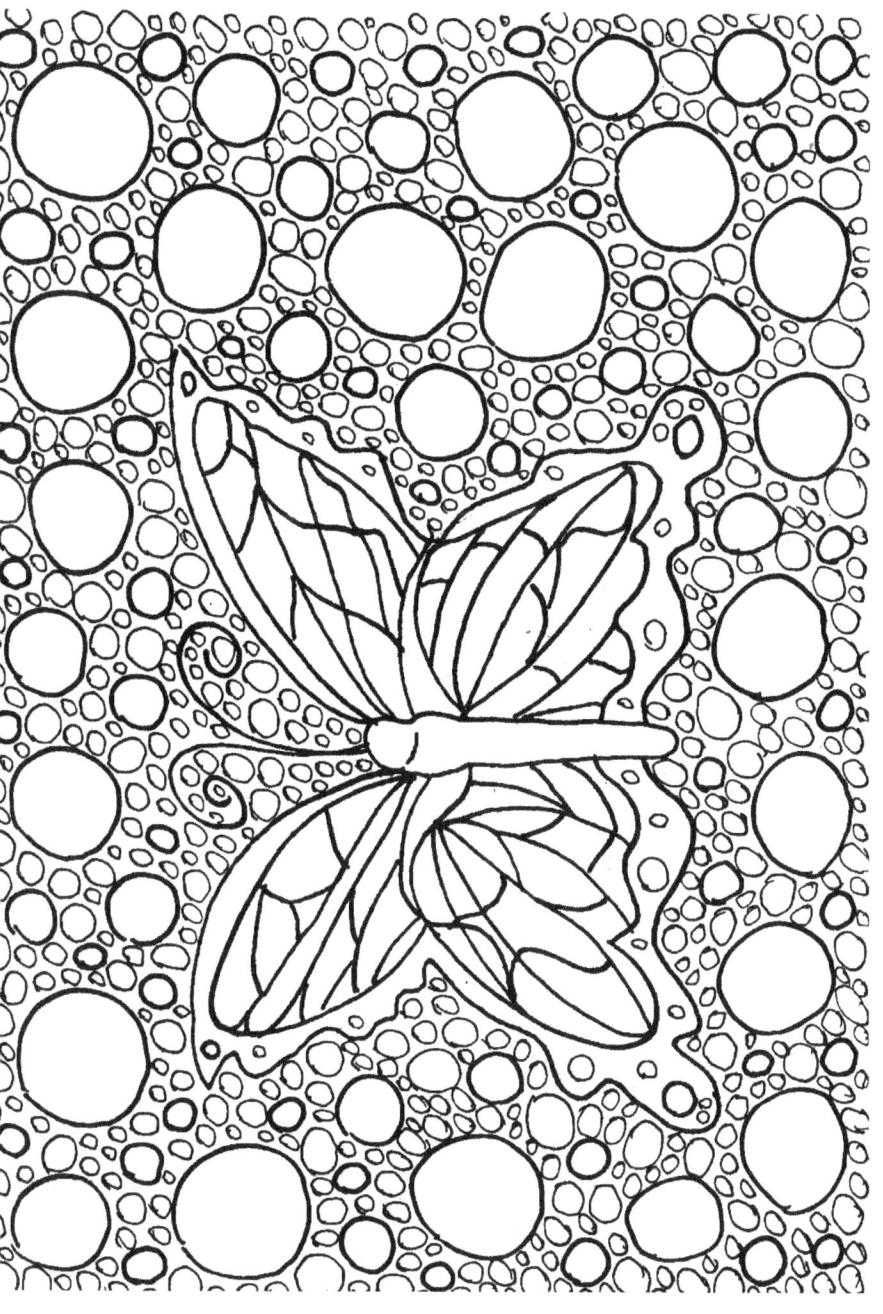

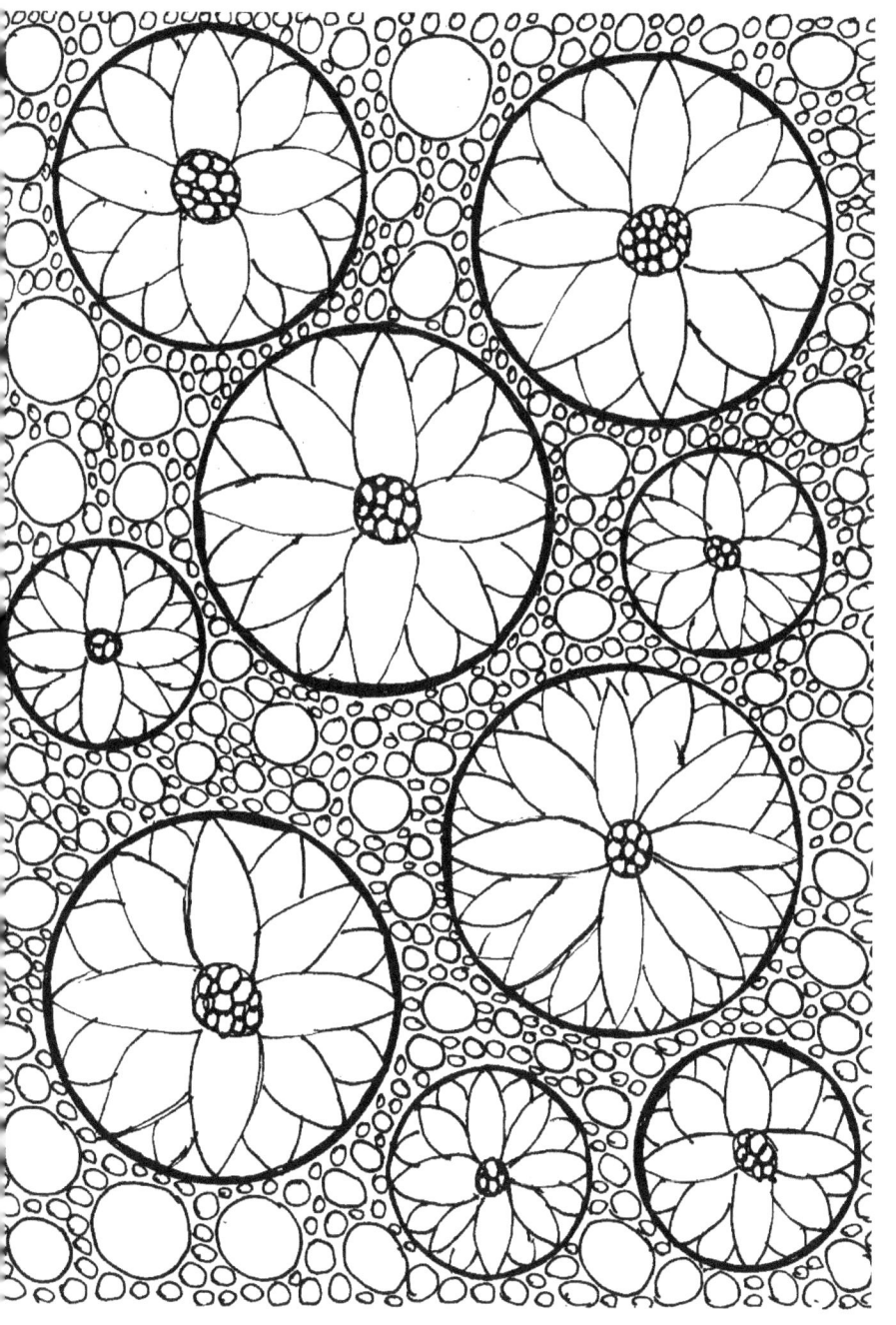

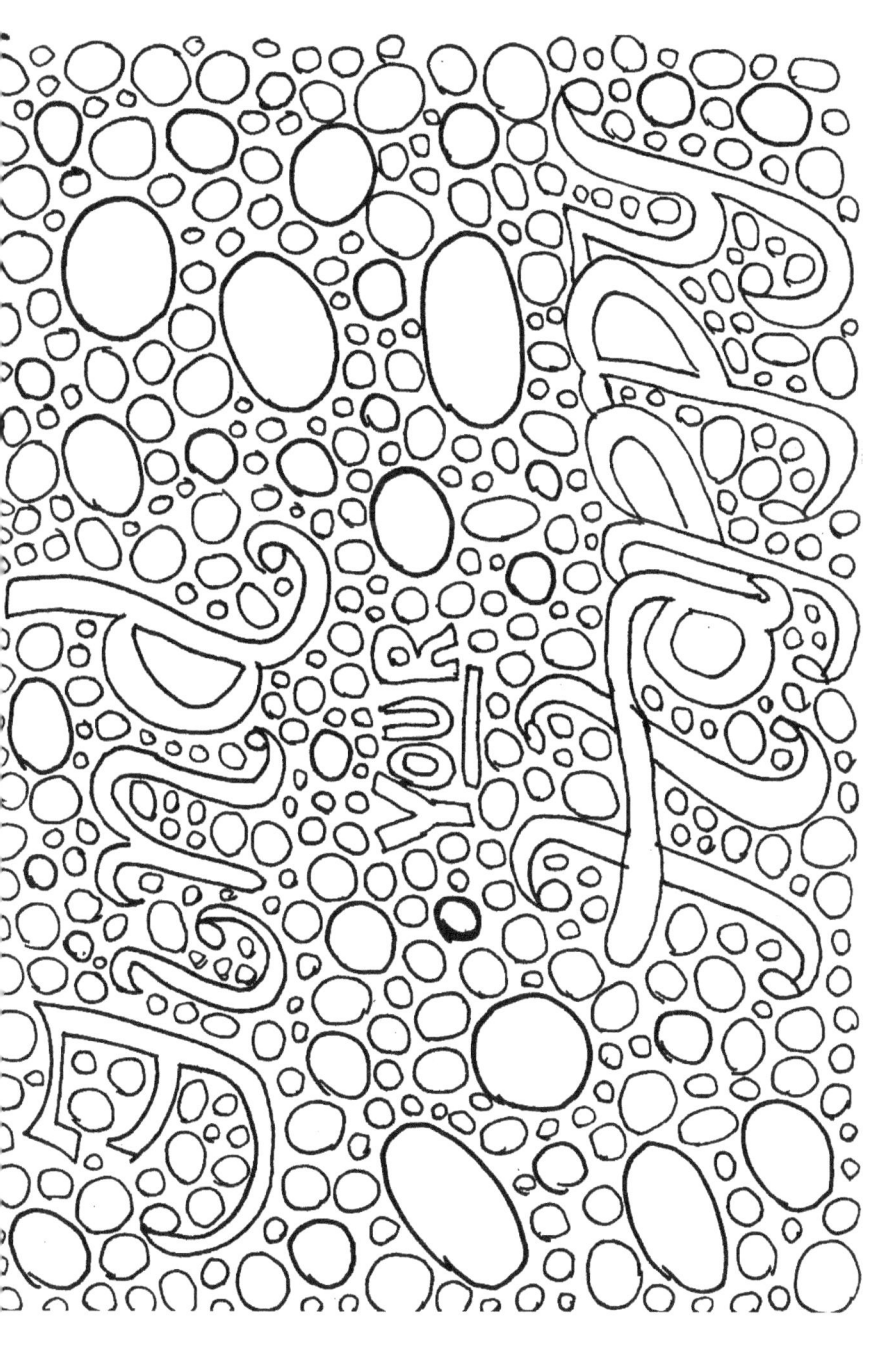

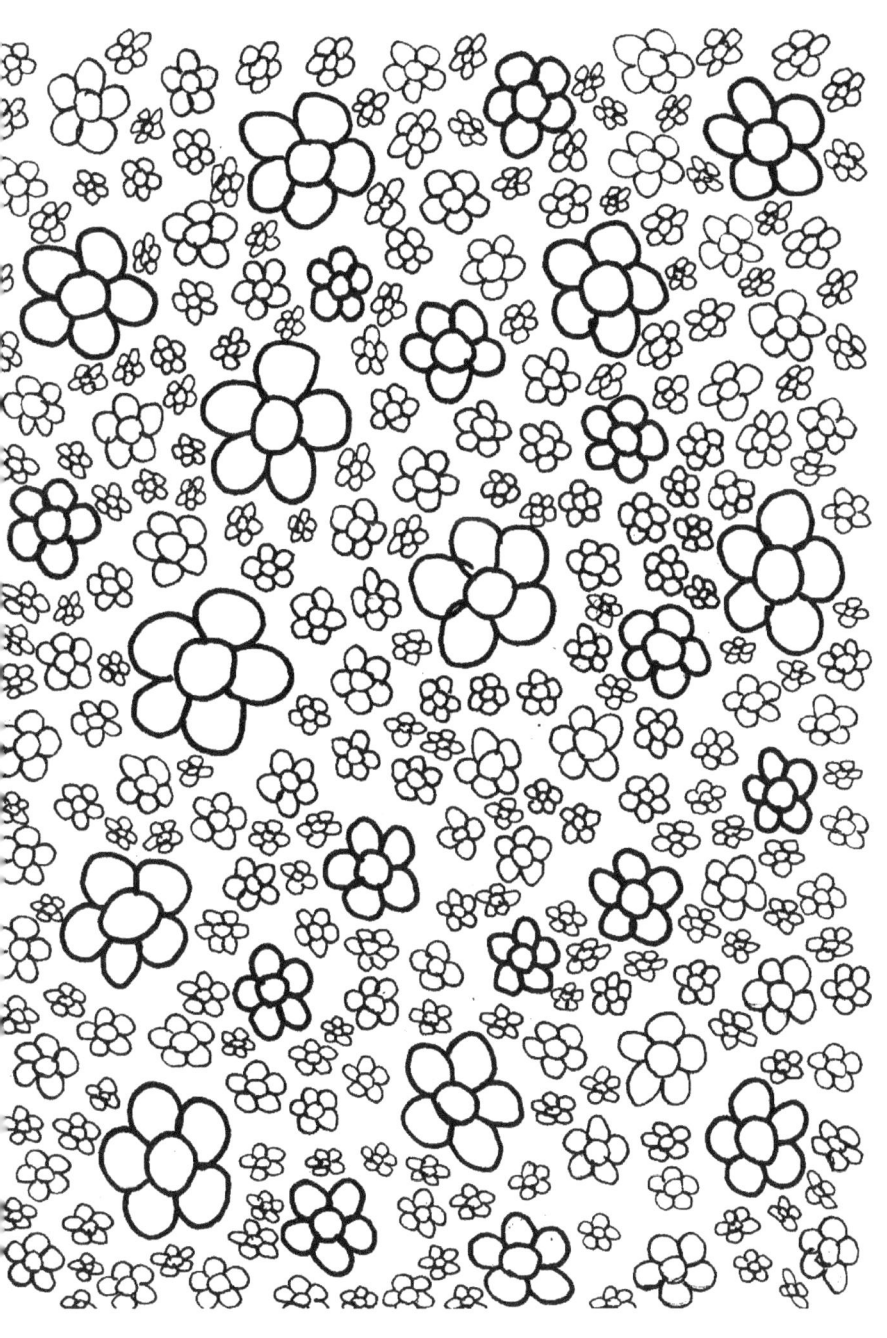

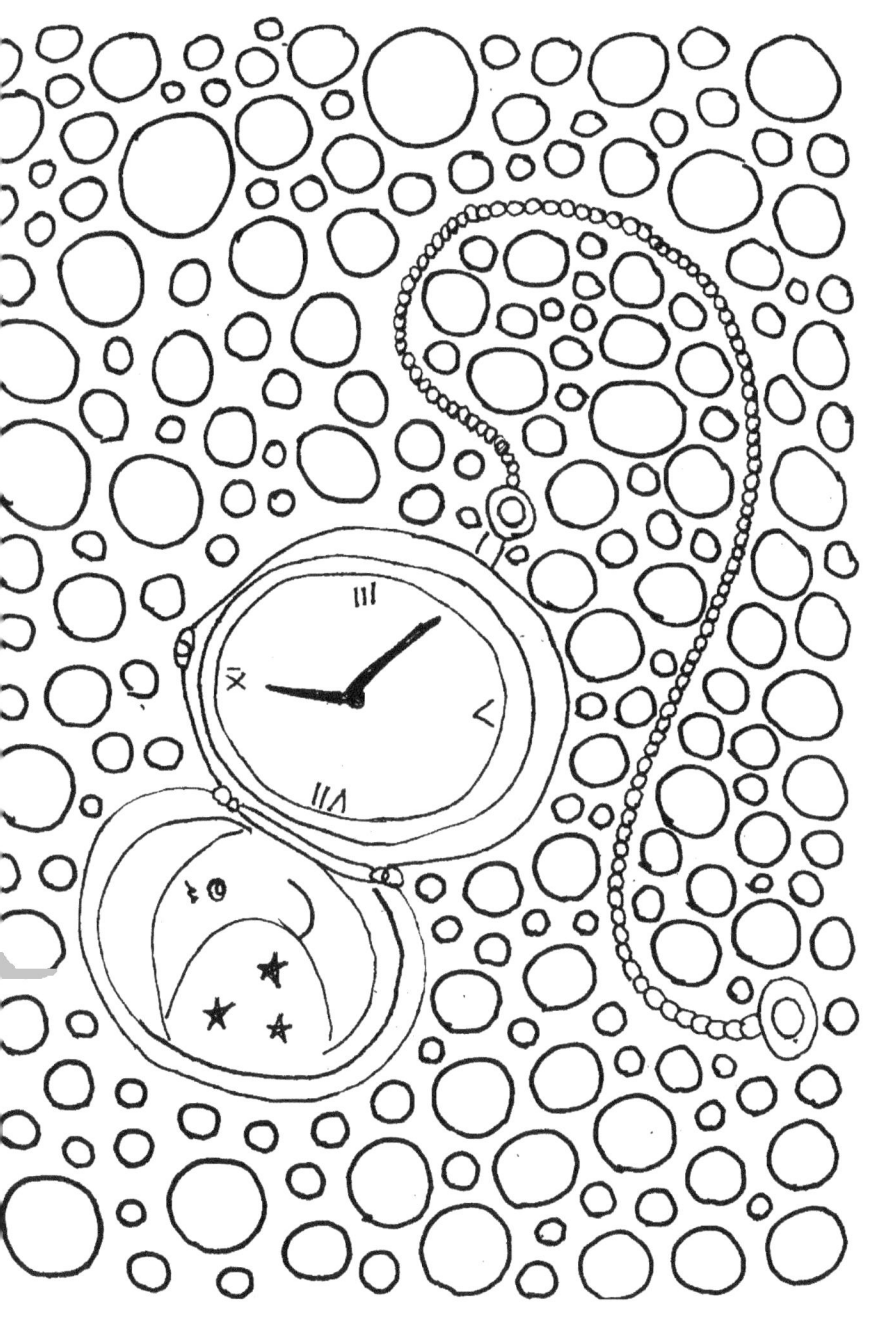

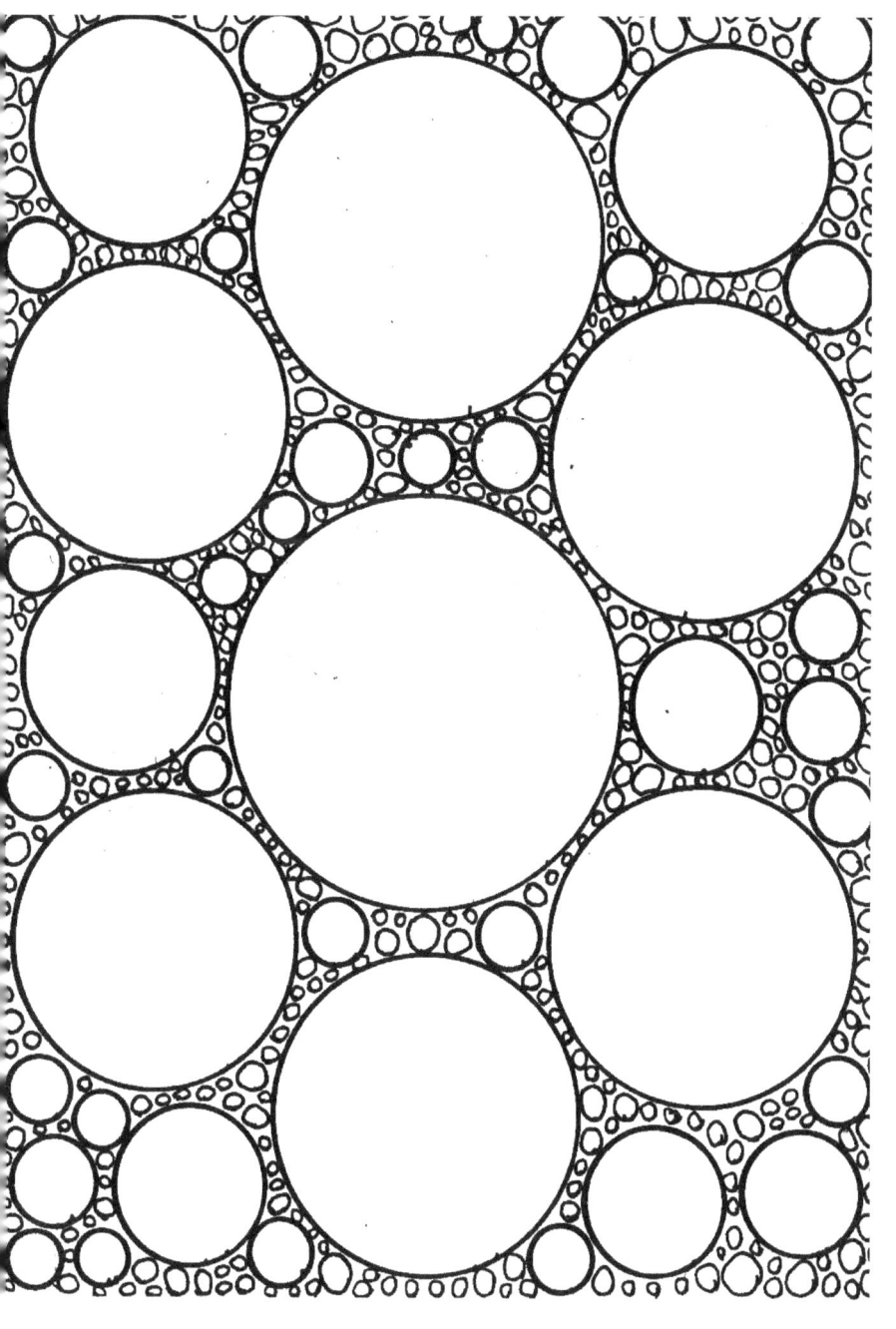

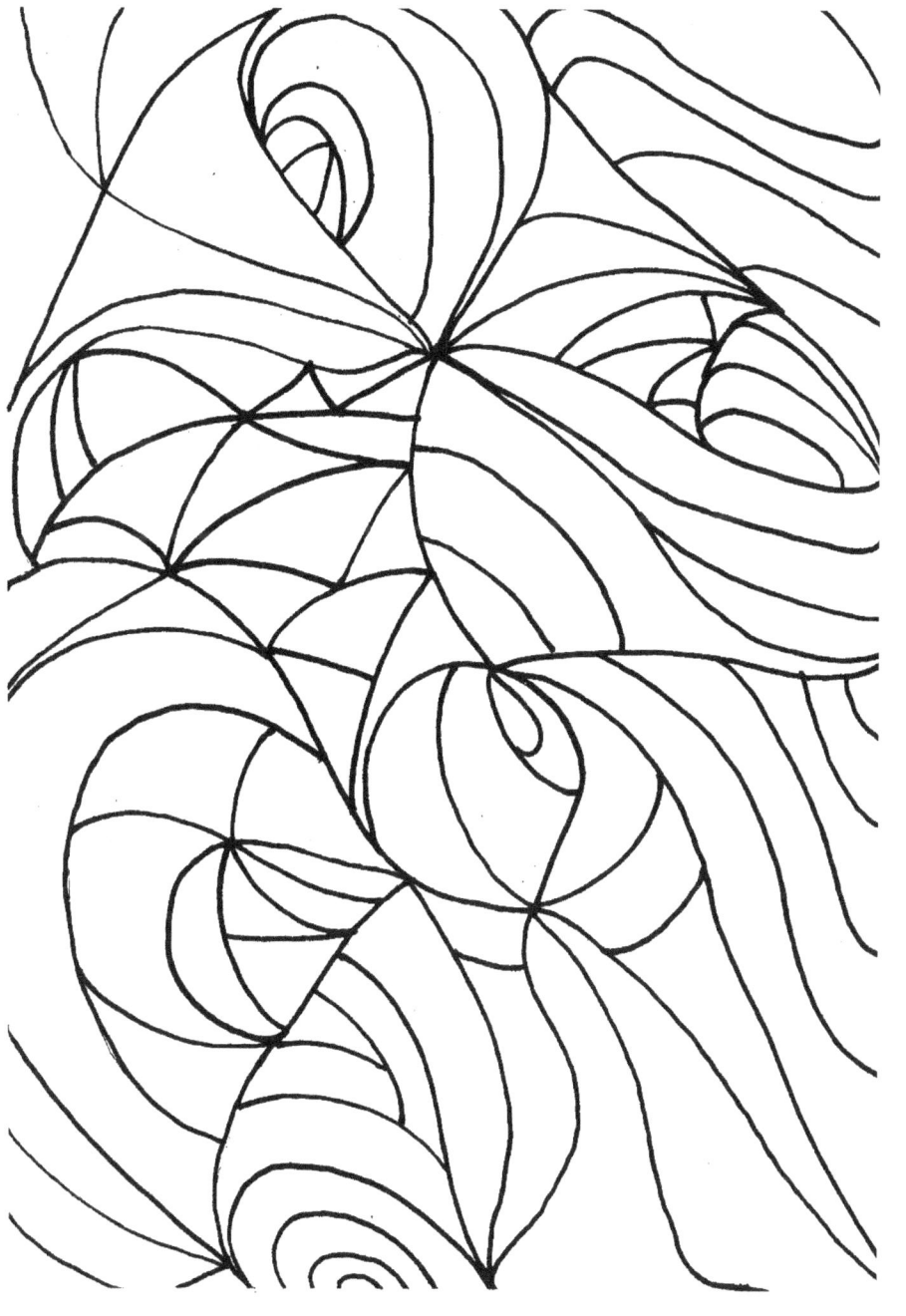

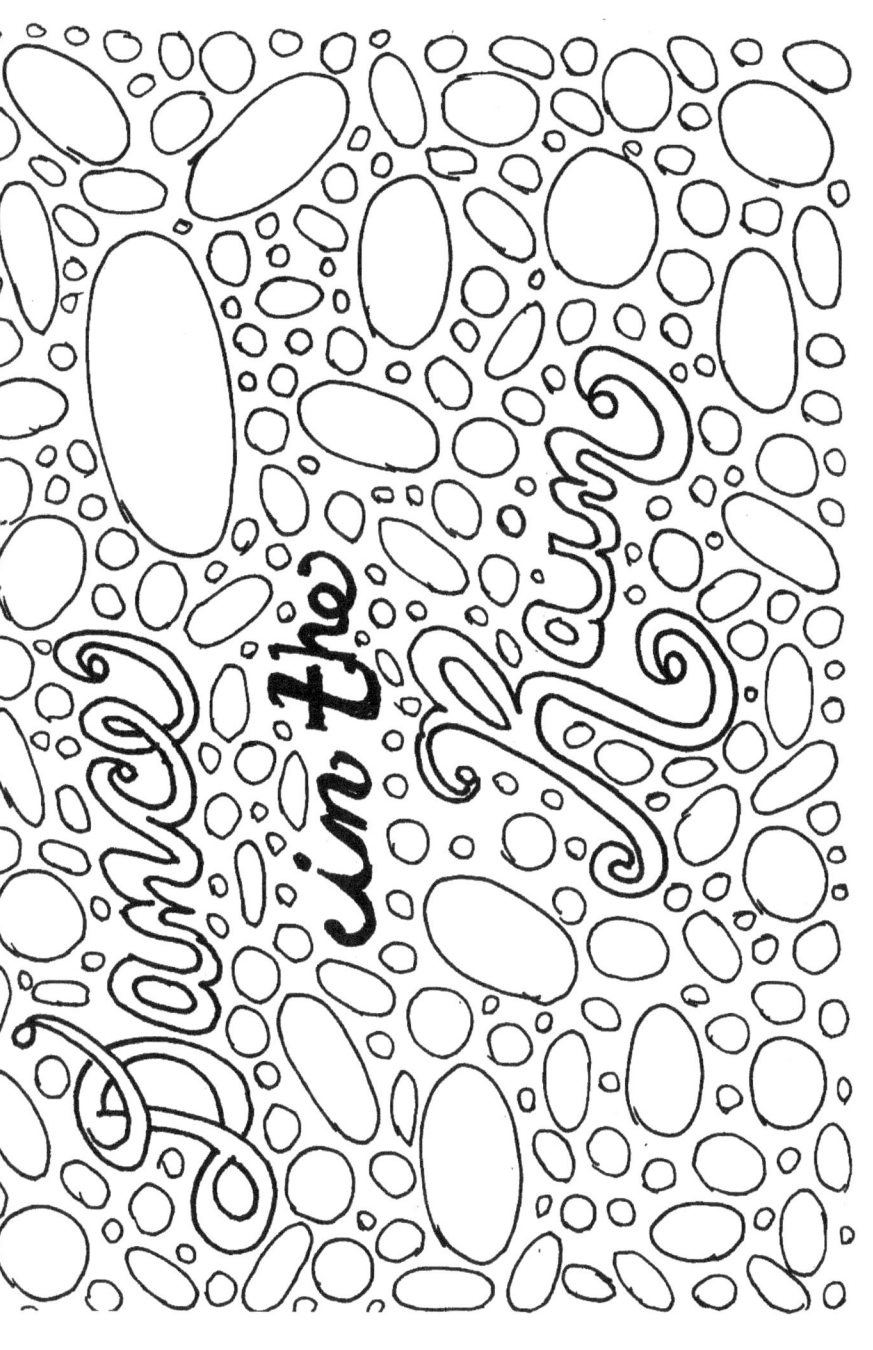

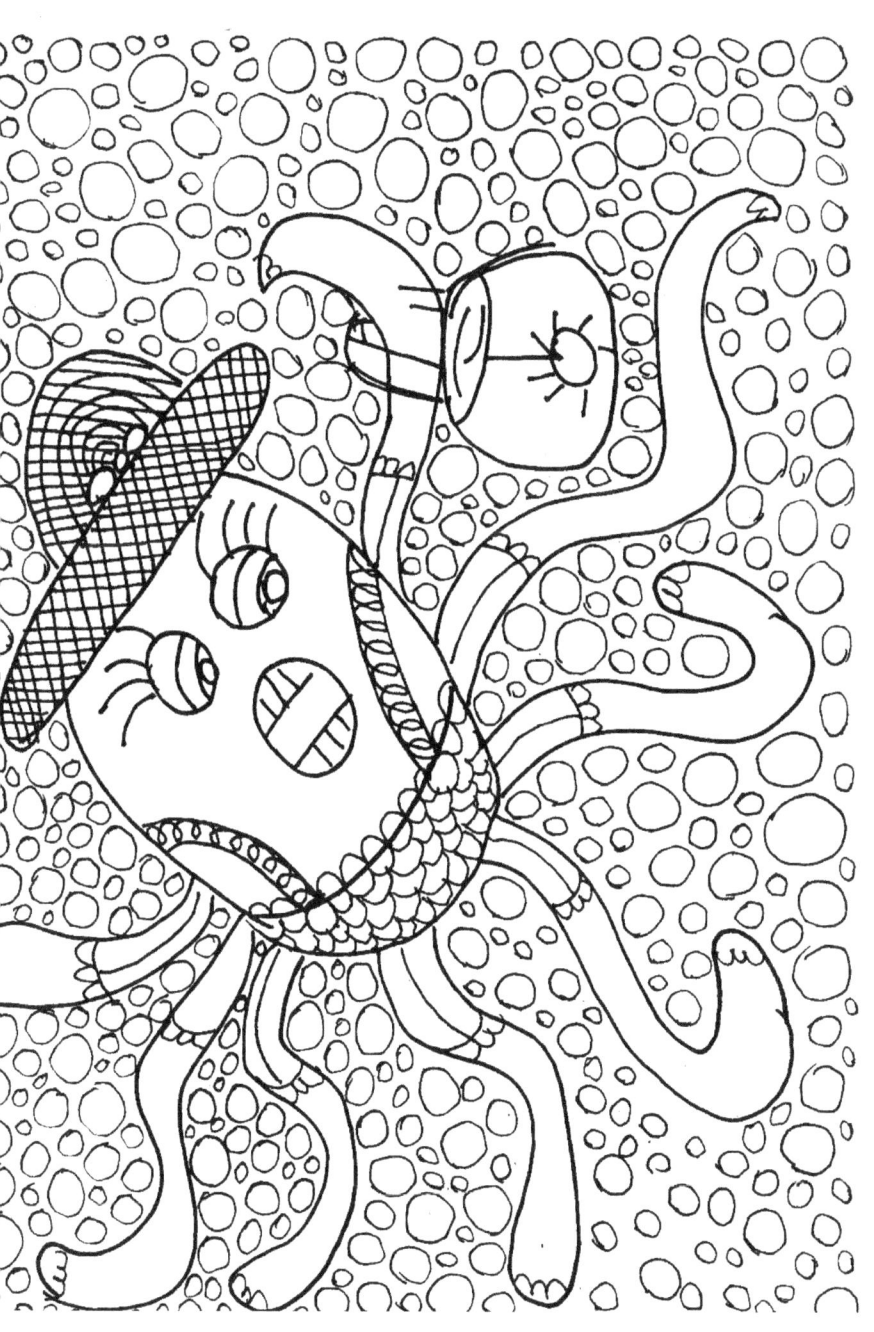

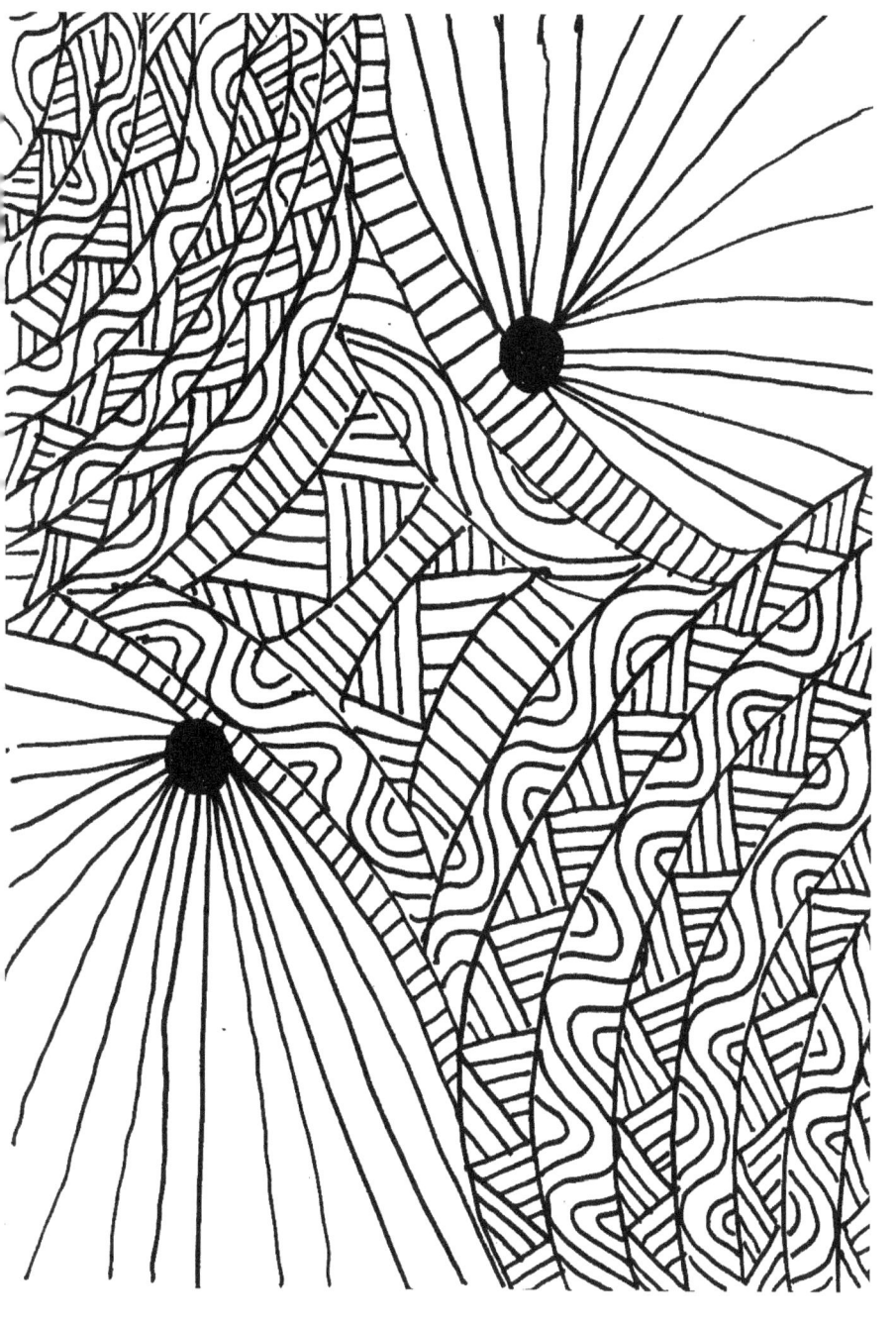

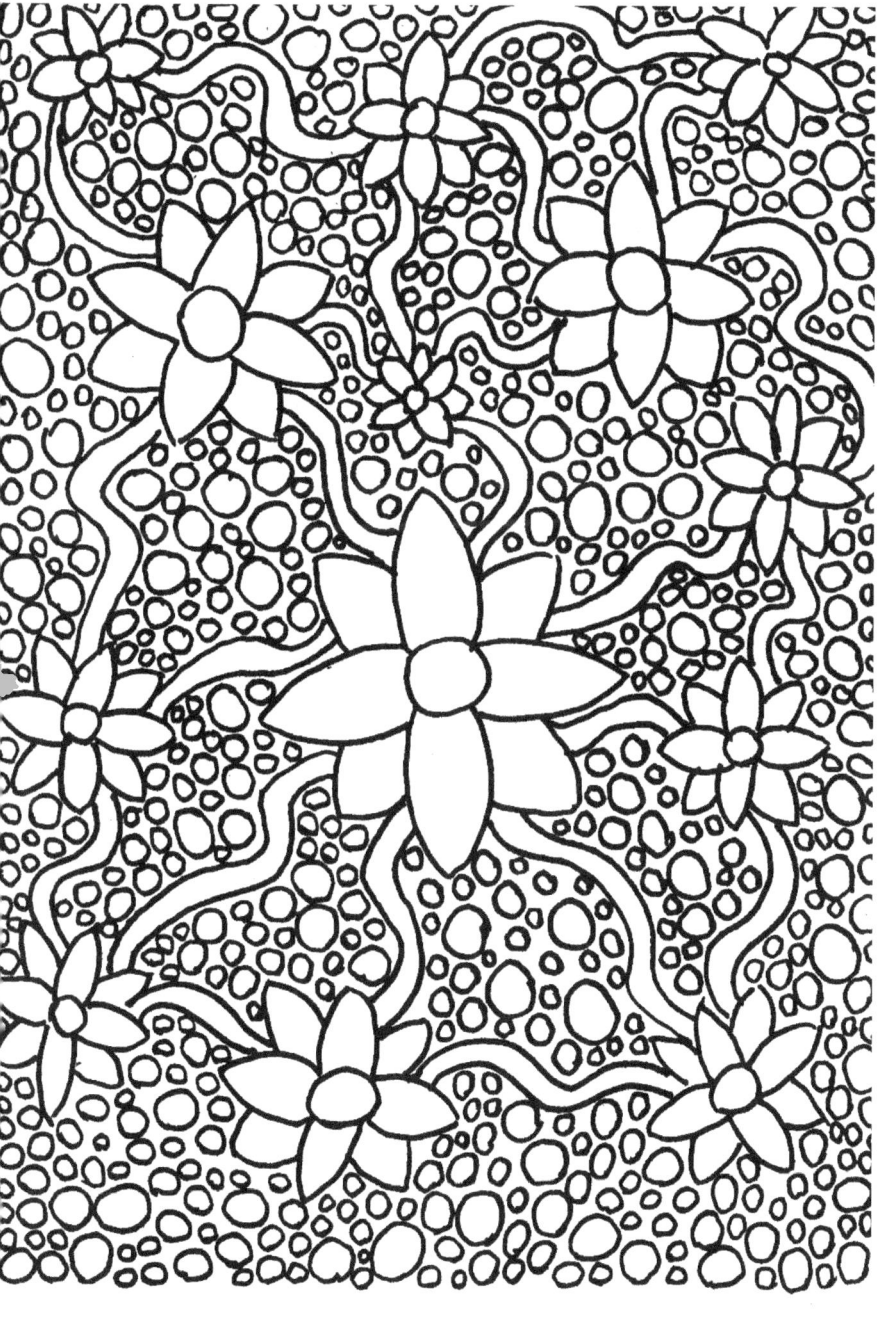

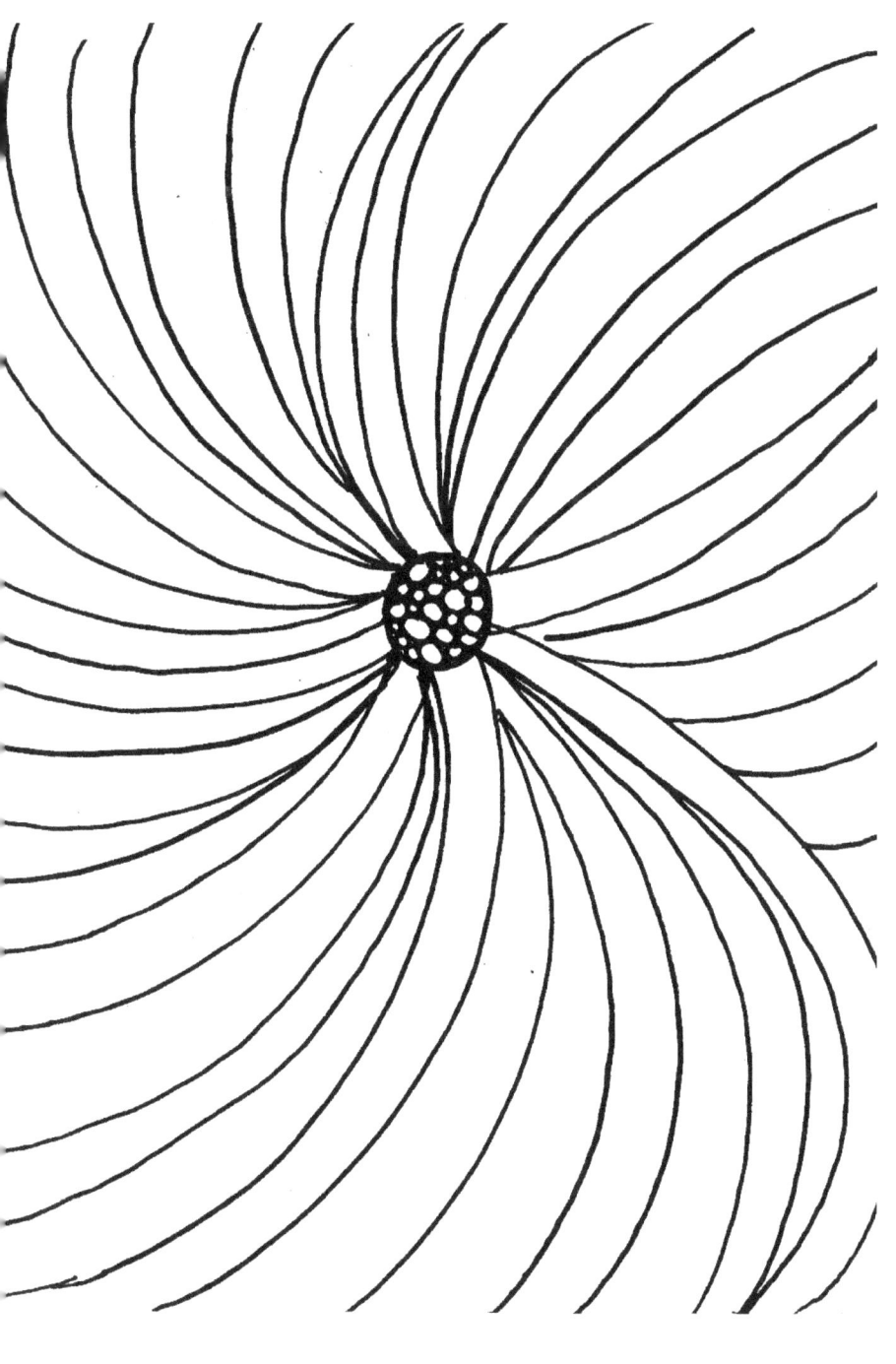

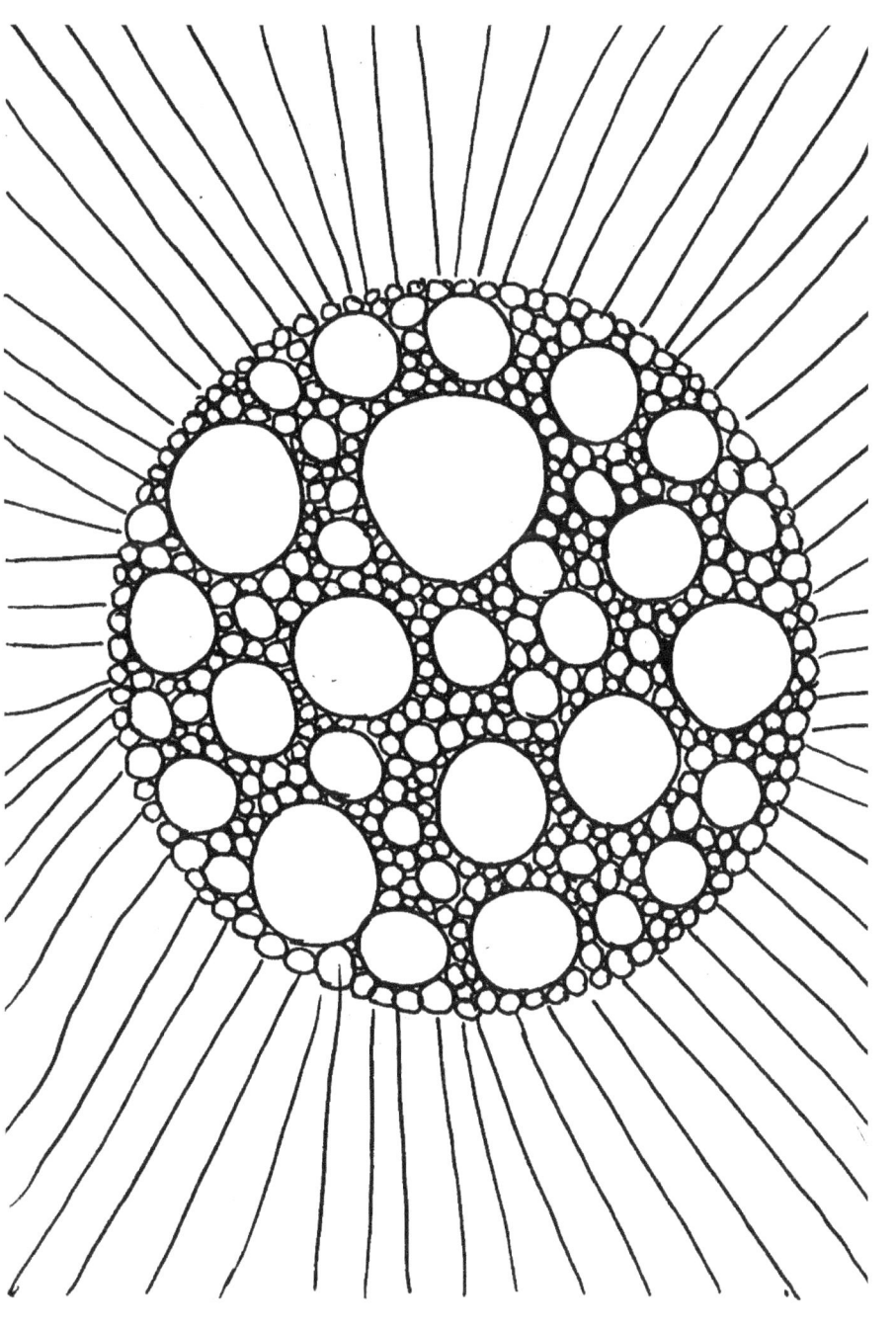

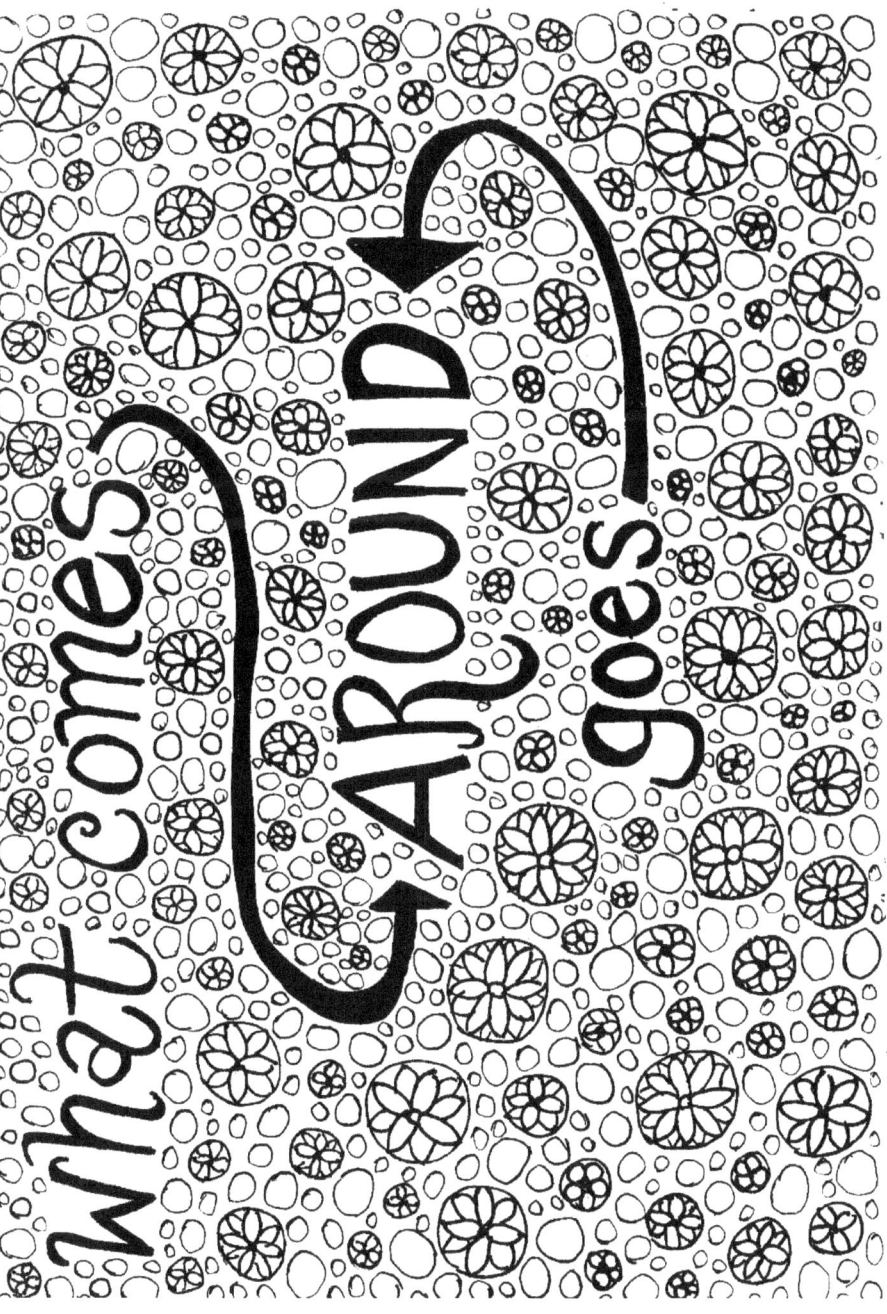

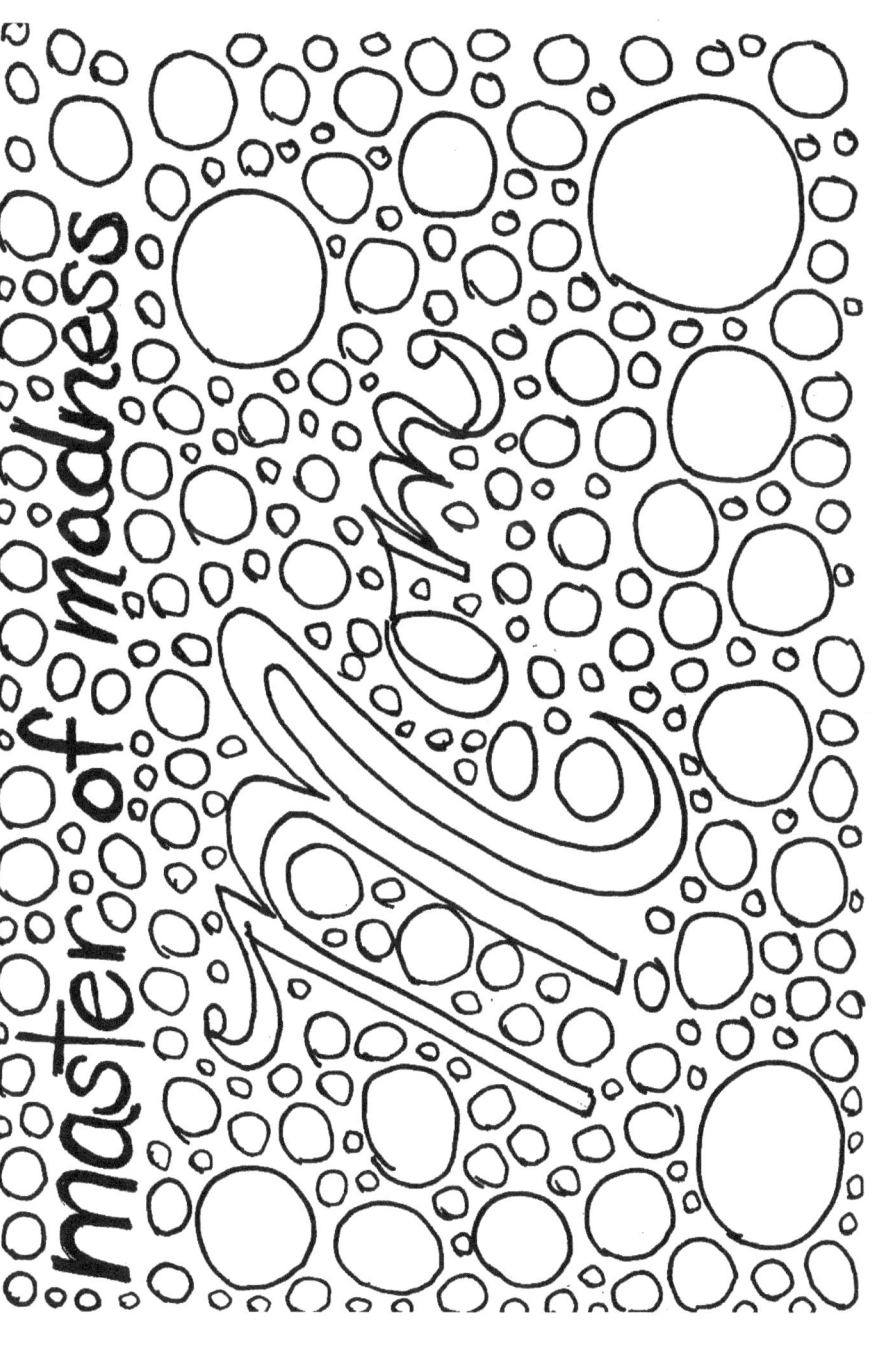

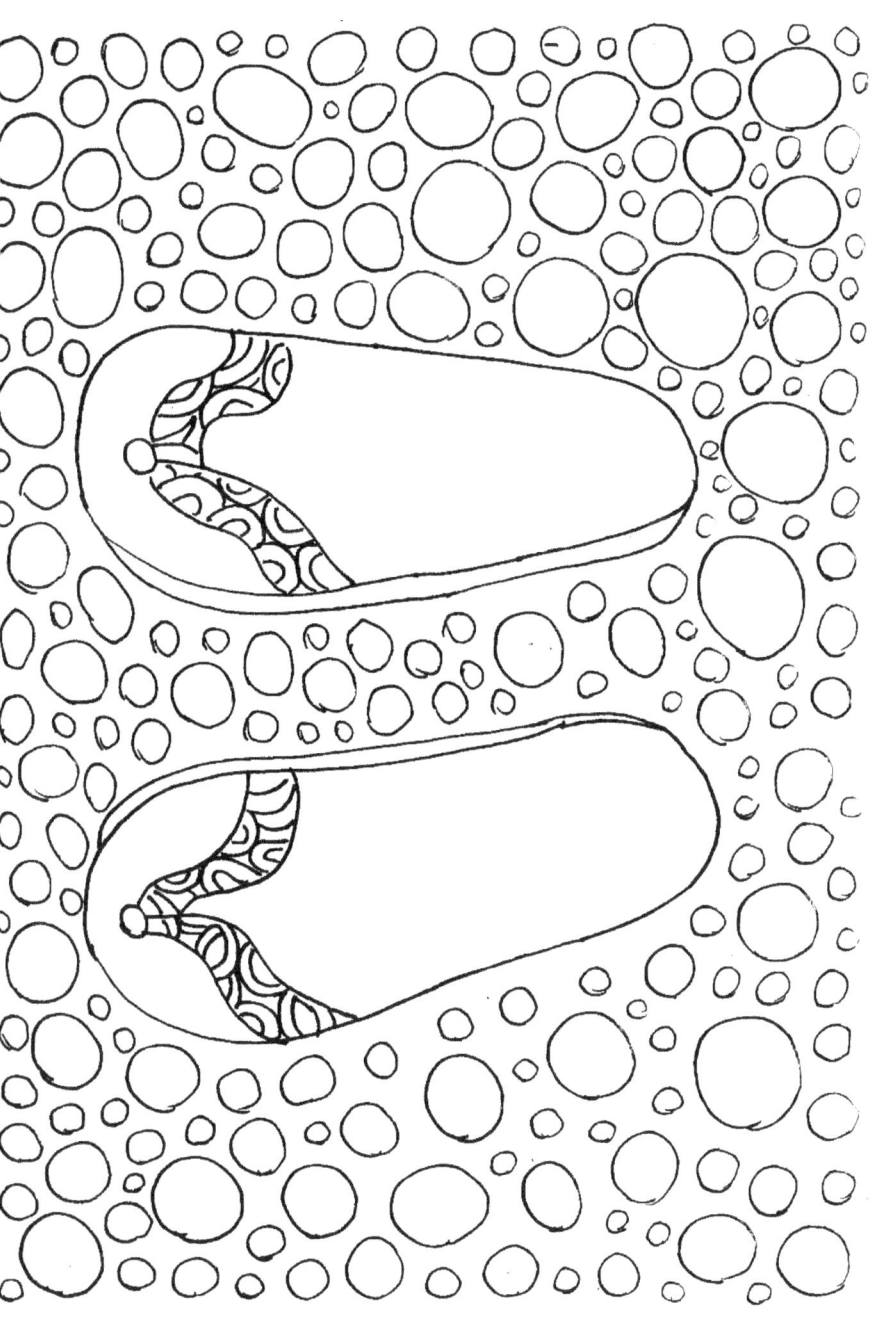

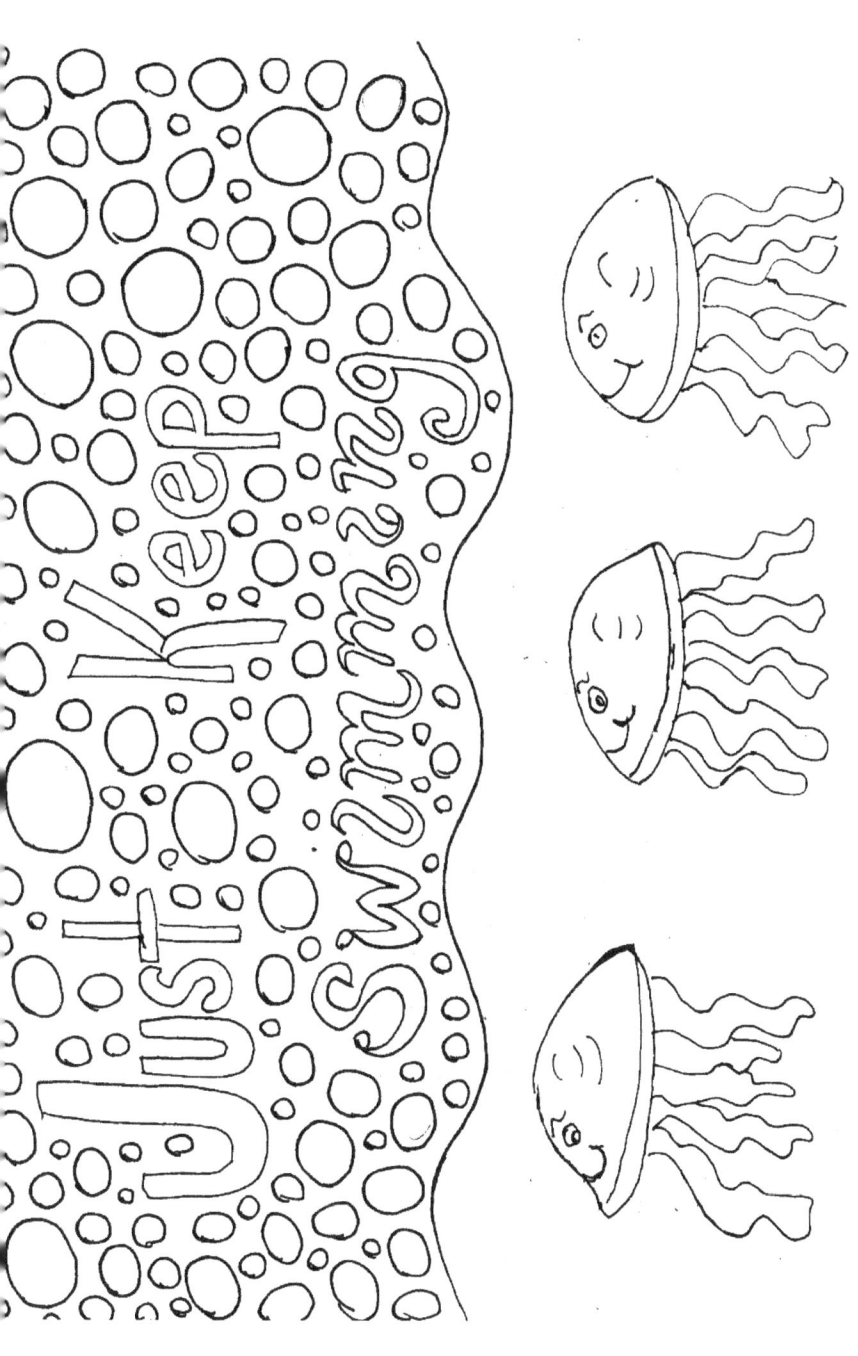

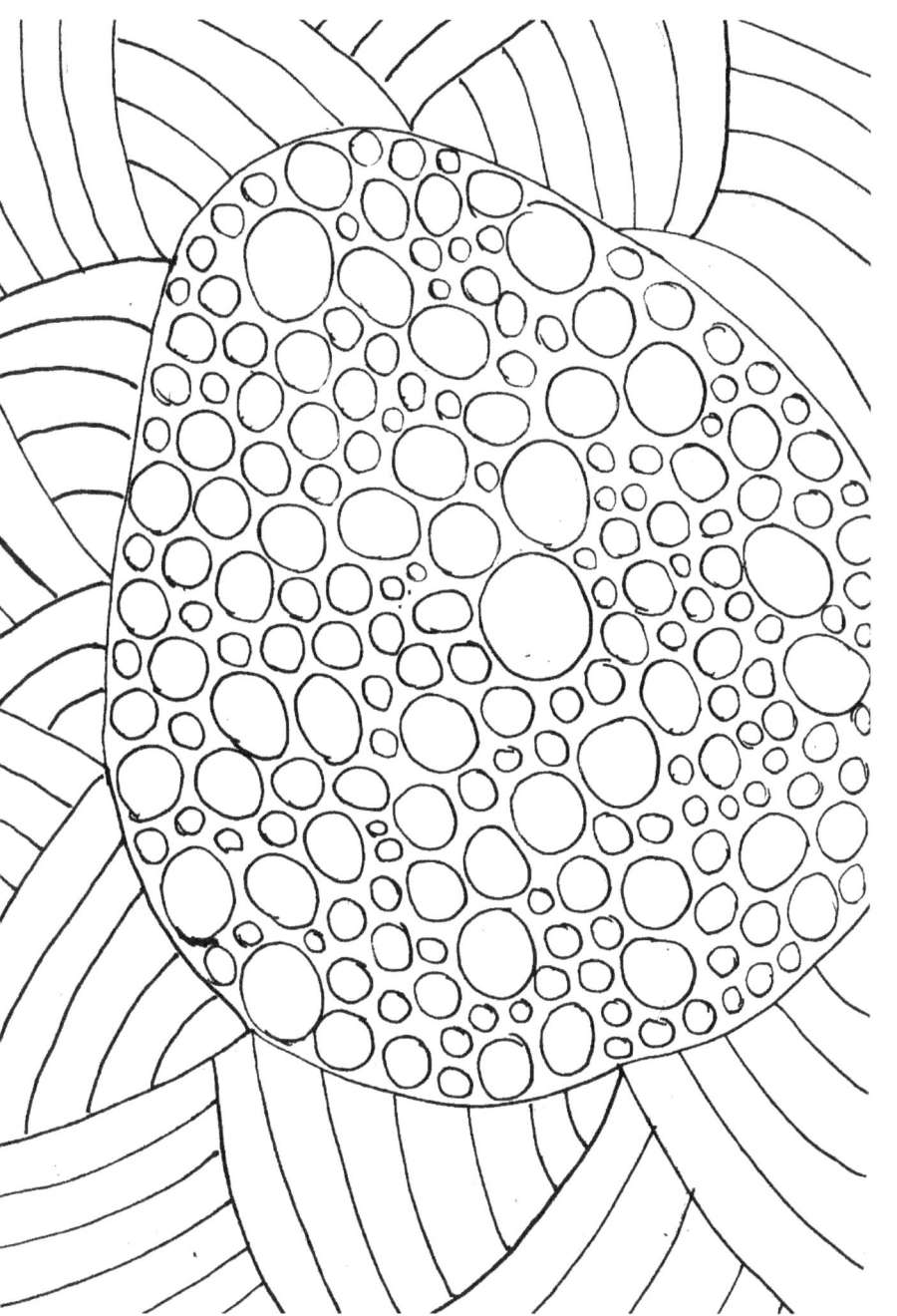

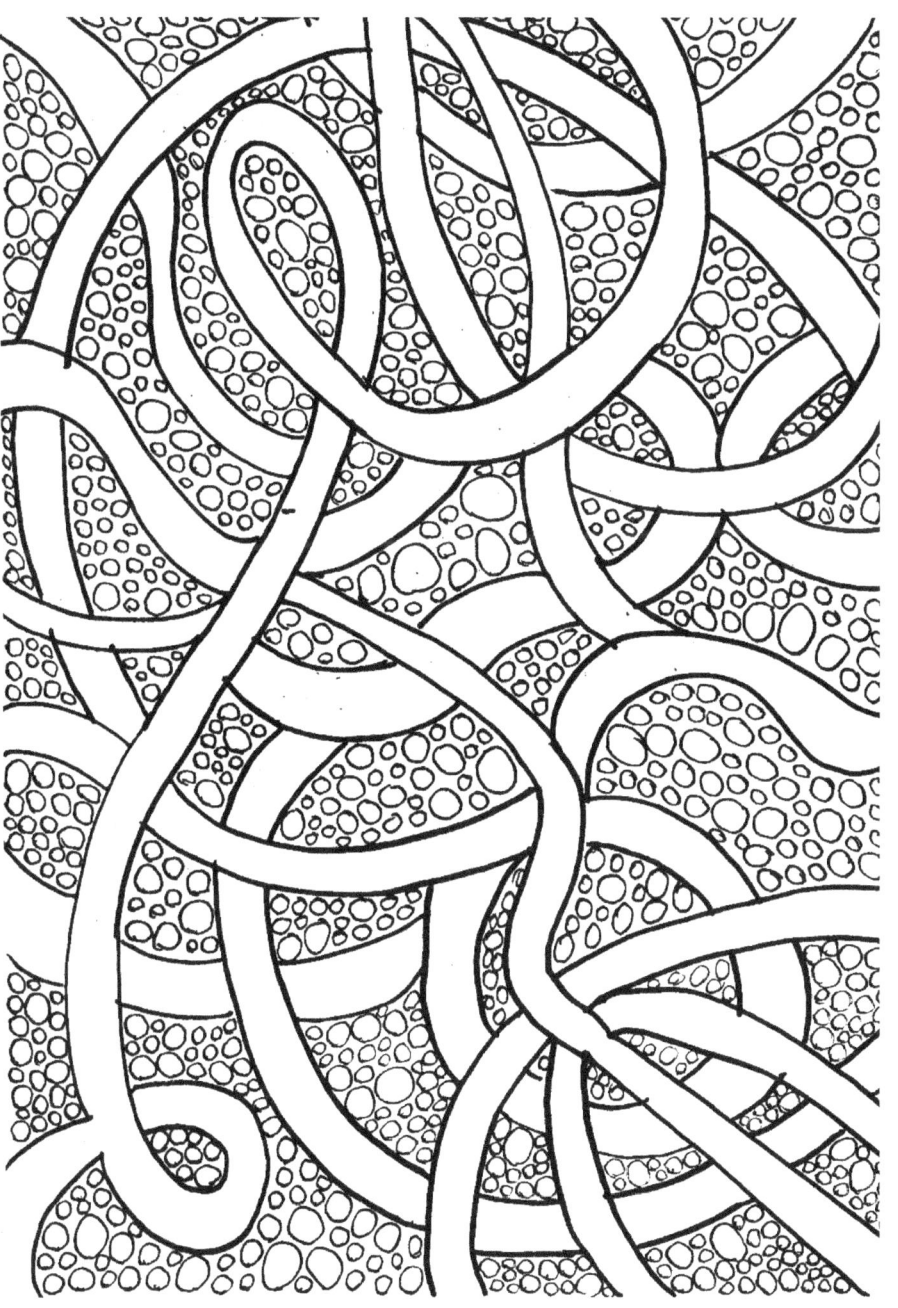

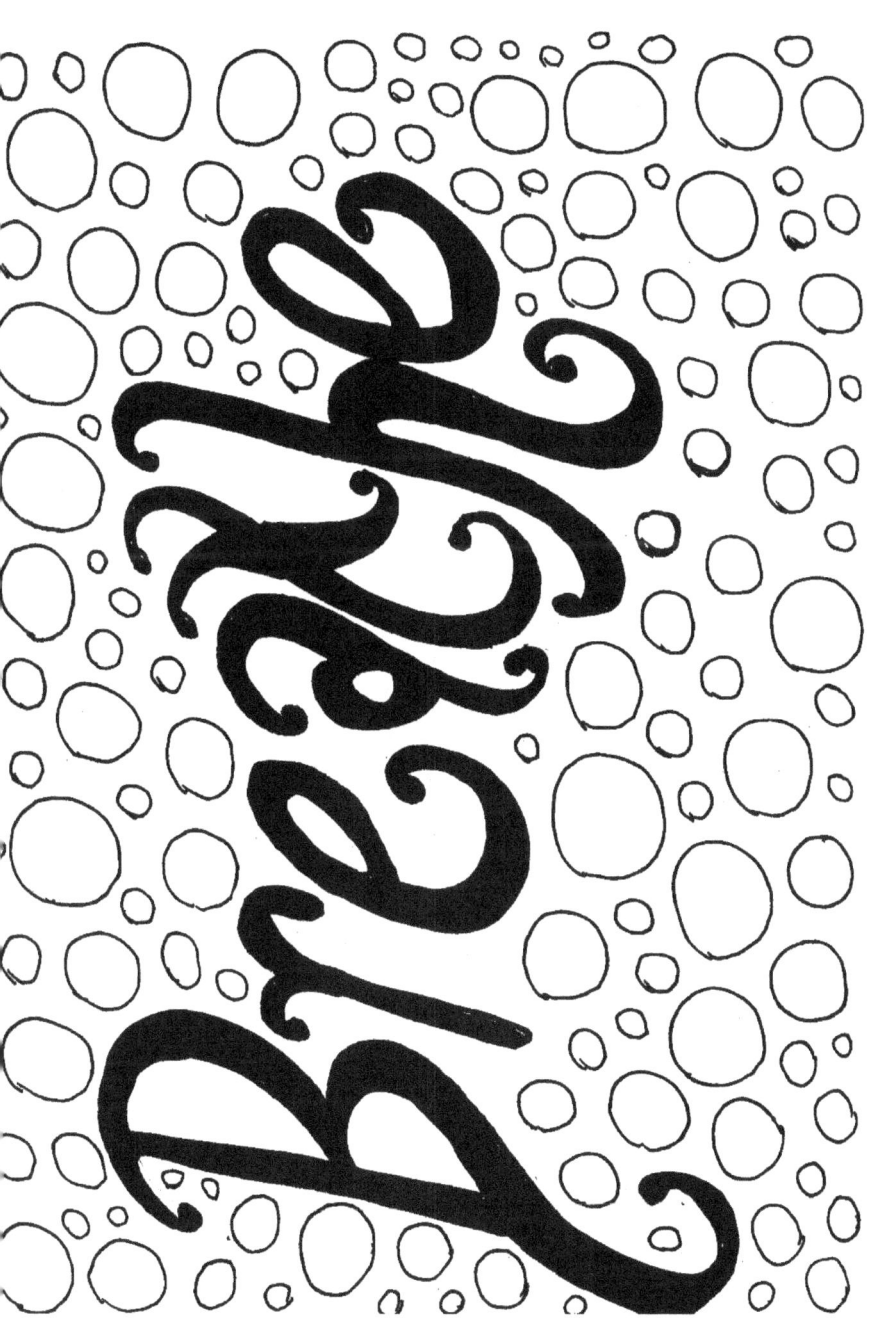